KUMBHA

Kumbha
The Traditionally Modern Mela

REVISED AND UPDATED

Nityananda Misra

BLOOMSBURY
NEW DELHI · LONDON · OXFORD · NEW YORK · SYDNEY

BLOOMSBURY INDIA
Bloomsbury Publishing India Pvt. Ltd
Second Floor, LSC Building No. 4, DDA Complex, Pocket C – 6 & 7,
Vasant Kunj New Delhi 110070

BLOOMSBURY, BLOOMSBURY INDIA and the Diana logo are trademarks of
Bloomsbury Publishing Plc

First published in India 2019
This revised edition published 2025

Copyright © Nityananda Misra 2019, 2025
Nityananda Misra has asserted his right under the Indian Copyright Act to
be identified as the Author of this work

Images © Uttar Pradesh Tourism, Wikimedia Commons (Rursus),
and Shutterstock (ravi090 and pratyush085p)

All rights reserved. No part of this publication may be reproduced or
transmitted in any form or by any means, electronic or mechanical,
including photocopying, recording or any information storage or retrieval
system, without the prior permission in writing from the publishers

Bloomsbury Publishing Plc does not have any control over, or responsibility
for, any third-party websites referred to or in this book. All internet
addresses given in this book were correct at the time of going to press. The
author and publisher regret any inconvenience caused if addresses have
changed or sites have ceased to exist, but can accept no responsibility for
any such changes

ISBN: PB: 978-9-3613-1514-5; eBook: 978-9-3884-1412-8

2 4 6 8 10 9 7 5 3 1

Typeset in Charis SIL and Chanakya Sanskrit by Nityananda Misra
Printed and bound in India by Replika Press Pvt Ltd

Bloomsbury Publishing Plc makes every effort to ensure that the papers
used in the manufacture of our books are natural, recyclable products made
from wood grown in well-managed forests. Our manufacturing processes
conform to the environmental regulations of the country of origin

To find out more about our authors and books visit www.bloomsbury.com
and sign up for our newsletters

To Shivani

"punarehi"

Contents

Foreword by Dr David Frawley	ix
Preface	xv
Notes to the Reader	xxi
1 Introduction	1
2 Venues and Dates	17
3 Organization	33
4 Sadhus	61
5 *Kalpavasis* and *Tirthayatris*	87
6 New-age Hindu Movements	103
7 Literature, Arts, and Music	115
8 Commerce and Technology	129
9 Diversity and Inclusivity	143
10 The Immortal Mela	163
11 Personal Experiences	173
12 Kumbha 2025	201
Appendix	207
Bibliography	213
About the Author	217

Foreword

Kumbha: Humanity's Greatest Gathering

India's Kumbha Mela is the largest, oldest, and the most colourful spiritual and religious gathering in the world, attended by tens of millions of pilgrims and many thousands of yogis, babas, swamis, and sadhus. It is an event of incomparable magnitude, vast ancient traditions, special mystical visions, and contact with higher consciousness by many of its devoted pilgrims that affords it the aura of another dimension of reality altogether.

One could call the Kumbha the greatest human gathering on the face of the Earth and one that occurs on a regular basis, with the Melas happening every three years in different parts of India. Yet, it is not just a wonderful display; the Kumbha is a deeply reverential event such as no other country has been able to preserve or sustain. There is nothing comparable to this magnitude, frequency, or antiquity in any other religion or culture. It is not just a matter of a special day but a set of celebrations going on for up to two months.

In our new global media and travel era, more people from India and abroad are visiting this unique gathering than ever before. The Kumbha has become the most important event that represents mystical India for all to see—showcasing India's ancient and very different yogic culture that the world is only now slowly beginning to discover again in the dawning planetary age, as the practice of Yoga has now spread worldwide.

The Kumbha was originally devised as a special spiritual event to allow the masses to meet with the great gurus and sadhus of many different lineages and *sampradayas* of India, who are otherwise hard to access and are living in different parts the country—often in remote locations that are difficult to reach. At the Kumbha, the sadhus and their disciples appear in public and share their work, teachings, and practices with the society as a whole.

All of the Hindu Dharma comes out for this magnificent event, with its many sects, branches, and all of its deity and philosophical lines represented in their full expression. It is the best place to experience what Hinduism is in all of its depth, diversity, and very different views of life and humanity. It reveals Hinduism as the Sanatana Dharma, the universal and eternal tradition as it was originally formulated to be. The Kumbha easily becomes an experience beyond time, place, person, or culture to affirm our magical connections with the entire universe—known and unknown.

The Kumbha Mela Experience

Sadly, much of the media, particularly in the West, prefer to sensationalize this extraordinary event and highlight its difficulties or what it regards as unusual types of behaviour. Certainly, the Kumbha Mela challenges our mindset as to what spirituality has to offer, but isn't that what we need to do—to go beyond our limitations and preconceptions? Such diversity of holy men and holy women and sacred practices cannot be experienced anywhere else. The Kumbha takes us beyond our current world situation to another time and civilization when human beings were rooted in the sacred. The Kumbha stretches our limits as to what is holy, extending it to the whole of life and nature.

In the Hindu thought, the universe is a creation, or to put it better, a manifestation of *ananda* or immortal bliss and joy as it overflows in every possible way—from the unbound eternal to the circumscribed realms of time. Even our sorrows are but incomplete bits of *ananda* looking for the greater connections in order to turn into joy. That effusive spirit of *ananda* underlies and permeates the Kumbha Mela and its celebrations.

The Kumbha connects us from the Earth and the rivers to the transcendent beyond all manifestation. The Kumbha is famous for its sacred baths or *snanas* in the sacred rivers, such as Mother Ganges. For the Hindus, it is not some mere single baptism to change one's faith, but a continual set of sacred baths to renew one's connection with the Divine, embracing the mountain gods and river goddesses, the plants and animals, and our own inner Self that is one with all.

Our purpose in life is not just to make money, gain adulation or assume power in the outer world and its human-centred affairs. Our soul's purpose is to take our consciousness beyond the limitations and opinions of the mind. Our true purpose is to discover a new sense of wonder, mystery, and amazement, just like the Kumbha Melas embody.

There are many other such celebrations and pilgrimages in India. But the Kumbha is the most important of all of these. Today, we need to honour and preserve such an extraordinary festival. The Kumbha Mela should be respected as a key component of our global spiritual heritage that cannot be circumscribed by any belief, institution, person, or creed.

The Kumbha was first brought to light to the global audience in Paramahansa Yogananda's acclaimed work *Autobiography of a Yogi* where it captured mystical accounts of gurus, sadhus, saints, and sages. Yogananda describes how his own guru Sri Yukteswar met his *paramguru*, the immortal Babaji, at the Kumbha. This has become the archetypal story of spiritual search in the world for both those in the West as well as those in India.

We all need to discover our sacred Kumbha Mela or meetings with the great masters. While this can be an inner experience, it can also be an outer experience at the Kumbha. In fact, it can be an inner and an outer experience at the same time.

The Book

Concise and clear information on the Kumbha Mela is difficult to find in an accessible English idiom, as it is easier for writers to highlight only a side of this vast event. In this regard, the book *Kumbha: The Traditionally Modern Mela* by Nityananda Misra is complete and comprehensive, examining the Kumbha from every possible perspective—starting with its ancient history to its modern adaptation, growing recognition, and the personal experiences of those who have attended it.

On one level, the book forms an important reference guide that tells the reader all they need to know about the Kumbha in a practical and detailed manner: its locations, organization, timings, and procedures involved, including the different types of sadhus and the monastic orders that they represent. Yet, on another level, the book reflects both a personal and a collective inspiration, an inner connection with the spirit of the Kumbha, bringing it alive for the reader in all its depth and breadth. The author especially explores the cultural aspects and connections of the Kumbha by extending it to literature, art, and music, which unfold the values and insights of India's great dharmic civilization.

Like many such sacred events, the origins of the Kumbha are hidden in the darkness of time as the author notes. The Kumbha is reflected in the arcane symbolism of Hindu texts that are accessible by only a few, much less understood. The Kumbha is woven into Hinduism's sacred geography that delineates the region of India from Kanyakumari to the Himalayas by sacred sites, temples, rivers, and mountains. It is marked by Hinduism's unique calendar of sacred time and religious events relative to the signs of the zodiac and the planetary movement of Jupiter, making it a cosmic event.

In our new planetary era of ecological concerns and the honouring of global spirituality, the Hindu tradition with its great abundance of practices has a special place in preserving our global spiritual heritage. The Kumbha Mela is the crown jewel of the Hindu experience—of being in harmony with the entire universe.

Such a collective pilgrimage of entering into the sacred waters of the universe reflects our highest human aspiration to one with the infinite and the eternal. We can all learn to appreciate the Kumbha and many of us can join it for a direct experience of our cosmic Self in the vision of the great gurus, rivers, and deathless streams of consciousness. The year of the

Kumbha, 2019, can have a special value for each one of us.

Kumbha: The Traditionally Modern Mela is an excellent study of the Kumbha from its mysterious origins to its current global prominence, looking forward to the Kumbha 2019 in Prayagraj, which has been returned to its traditional name from Allahabad, as Prayag indicates the confluence of rivers on which the Kumbha is placed. As such, the book can be regarded as a guidebook for the 2019 Kumbha, allowing us to prepare our minds and hearts for the next manifestation of the immortal Kumbha.

All those intending to visit this extraordinary event should read this inspiring book, if not travel with it to the Kumbha!

Dr David Frawley

(Pandit Vamadeva Shastri)

Acharya, Eminent Hindu Scholar, and Author of *What is Hinduism?*, *Arise Arjuna*, and *Awaken Bharata*

Preface

Hinduism is often called *Sanatana Dharma*, "the eternal practice or path". This path is eternal because it has evolved since time immemorial to subsume dramatic changes brought about by time, and has yet stayed true to its original Vedic spirit of moving together reflected in the *saṃgacchadhvaṃ saṃvadadhvam* mantra. With the world changing at an ever-increasing pace, Hindu traditions and practices continue to evolve as before, marrying the traditional and the modern in a mellifluous harmony. A living proof of this dynamic nature of Hinduism is the Kumbha Mela, which continues to modernize keeping pace with the times in the twenty-first century.

The Kumbha Mela is held at four places: Haridwar, Prayaga, Nashik-Tryambakeshwar, and Ujjain. At each of these four places, the fair is held after twelve years in general. The Ardha Kumbha is held halfway in the twelve-year interval at Haridwar and Prayaga. Each of these melas attracts crores of pilgrims, both sadhus and ordinary people, at a spectacular confluence of faith, piety, spirituality, urban planning, literature, arts, music, healthcare, commerce, science, and technology—all these united by a Hindu tradition. The Mela has been called "the greatest show on earth", "the largest pilgrimage on earth", and "the world's biggest festival". The Mela is much more than a show, a pilgrimage, or a festival—it is the greatest confluence of humanity celebrating the universal human values of love, peace, and coexistence.

Despite being so, the Kumbha Mela has not been given due importance in popular Indian and global culture for a long time. When I was in school in the 1990s, a reference to the Kumbha Mela among friends of my age would come up only when we joked about a twin or child who was separated or lost at a Kumbha Mela (a popular Bollywood theme). While this was the prevalent idea about the Kumbha among urban adolescents in India, the idea of the Kumbha among foreigners was limited to Naga sadhus. Popular culture in India reduced the Kumbha to a congregation where people went missing. Popular culture outside India trivialized the Kumbha to a festival of naked men. Mark Tully wrote of the 1989 Prayaga Kumbha, which he called "a triumph for the much-maligned Indian administrators" and a "greater triumph for the people of India", that the English press in India mostly reacted to the Mela with scorn. Times have since changed. Since the turn of the century, the Kumbha Mela has been a topic of several popular documentaries and shows. Recent Kumbha Melas have become too large to be ignored from a commercial viewpoint, and have seen innovative use of science and technology. In December 2017, the United Nations Educational, Scientific, and Cultural Organization (UNESCO) included the Kumbha Mela in its list of Intangible Cultural Heritage, a move hailed by Mahesh Sharma, the Union Minister of State for Culture. This was not an honour for the Kumbha Mela, the largest congregation on earth, but an honour for the UNESCO list itself. All this has possibly led to some sections of the English media in India and some English-speaking Indian elites now talking about the Kumbha Mela with pride. This is yet another example of Indians realizing something in India is great only when the West calls it so, or only when money or technology is involved.

The scale of the Kumbha Mela has steadily grown since India's independence in 1947, and the growth has accelerated since the dawn of the new millennium. The Mela has attracted more and more people from far and wide with time. In 1954, 50 lakh people (1.25% of India's population) attended the first Kumbha Mela at Prayaga after independence. This number rose to 1.5 crore (2.3% of India's population) in 1977, 2.90 crore (3.5% of India's population) in 1989, 5 crore (4.8% of India's population) in 2001, and 12 crore (9.8% of India's population) in 2013. The 2019 Ardha Kumbha, marketed as Kumbha by the authorities, saw an estimated 24 crore visitors (around 17.3% of India's population). Of these, around 10.3 lakh were foreign tourists. The 2021 Kumbha Mela in Haridwar was held during the COVID-19 pandemic and was, expectedly, a low-key affair with only around 90 lakh people attending it. Ignoring the small number of foreign tourists, it can be said that 1 in every 80 Indians attended the Kumbha in 1954, while 1 in every 10 attended the grand fair in 2013 and 1 in every 7 attended the semi-grand fair in 2019. Defying logic, an age-old religious and cultural tradition did not have to fight for survival but flourished in the new century. Today, with its awe-inspiring scale and universal appeal, the Kumbha Mela is arguably one of India's most magnificent cultural symbols.

Contrast these numbers of pilgrims for the Kumbha Mela with the number of pilgrims for the Hajj, the annual Islamic pilgrimage, which has ranged between 20 to 30 lakh from 2000 till date. The number of pilgrims on the main bathing day (*Mauni Amavasya*) in February 2013 at the Prayaga Kumbha was over three crore, ten times the total number of Hajj pilgrims over all five days during the annual Hajj held a few months ago in October 2012.

My first personal experience of the Kumbha Mela at Prayaga was vicarious, when one of my uncles participated in the 2001 Kumbha. In 2013, I participated in my first Kumbha Mela at the age of thirty, taking several days off from my job in the financial industry in Hong Kong to visit Prayaga, the "king of all *tirthas*". Later, I also attended the 2015 Simhastha Kumbha at Nashik-Tryambakeshwar, the 2016 Simhastha Kumbha at Ujjain and the 2019 Ardha Kumbha in Prayaga. What I experienced at these Kumbha Melas, especially the one in Prayaga, was the miraculous coming together—as if in perfect harmony—of technology and tradition, of commercialism and philanthropy, of the young and the old, of the rich and the poor, and of modern India and ancient India.

This book is on the this marriage of the traditional and the modern at the Kumbha Mela in the twenty-first century—traditional dates and elaborate planning, sacred land and modern makeshift infrastructure, homeless sadhus and jet-setters, travellers on foot and in SUVs, traditional *akharas* and new religious movements, *bhandaras* and fine dining, *kalpavasis* sleeping under the sky and foreigners in Swiss tents, crowded *shahi snanas* and solitary peaceful dips, *havanas* with Vedic hymns and contemporary bhajans, music on *ektaras* and music played with sound systems, *kathas* in Hindi and discourses in English, word of mouth and social media, oral accounts and video documentaries, eyewitnesses and CCTVs, tradition and modernity. The twelve chapters of the book represent the Mela's twelve-year cycle. The Kumbha Mela is an inclusive Hindu celebration of human life, and I devote two chapters to the inclusivity and the "never-say-die" spirit of the astounding Mela.

Like the contents of this book, my approach is also a mix of the traditional and the modern. I explain etymologies of important Sanskrit and Hindi terms and names relevant to the Kumbha along with their relevance in the modern context. I draw upon both traditional and contemporary accounts and literature on the Kumbha. I also supplement my research with my personal experiences at the multiple Kumbha Melas I have attended. The book's title reflects my own thought process which is "traditionally modern". I have made an effort to have something of value in this book for all participants of the Kumbha Mela—the traditional, the modern, and the traditionally modern.

The Kumbha Nagari, the temporary megacity at the Prayaga Kumbha Mela, is assembled from scratch within only two months before the Mela begins. The first edition of this book was similarly conceptualized, designed, written, typeset, and proofread in just two months. This revised edition is being brought out just before the 2025 Prayaga Kumbha.

Many people have helped me in writing this book. I am thankful to Praveen Tiwari and Nitin Valecha for their kind help in publishing the first edition. Nitin Valecha has been instrumental in bringing out the current (revised and updated) edition and I cannot thank him enough for this. Dr. Ramadhar Sharma of Patna taught me how to read the Swiss Ephemeris data with the *ayanamsha* correction, for which I am indebted to him. Thanks go to Prof. Ashish Verma of the Indian Institute of Science, Bengaluru, for kindly sharing his publications on the Kumbha Mela. I am much obliged to Richa Pandey who shared her experience of observing her grandparents perform the *kalpavasa* at the Magha and Kumbha Melas in Prayaga. Indavara Gayathri of Bengaluru shared her experience of the 2013 Prayaga Kumbha Mela, for which I fervently thank her. My mother, whose kindness and compassion knows no bounds, helped with the proofreading of the first edition's draft. Thanks are also due to Jaishree Ram Mohan for proofreading the changes for this revised edition at a very short notice. There are many others who have directly or indirectly contributed towards this book, and I thank all of them from the bottom of my heart.

It is impossible for any book to do justice to the Kumbha Mela. And it is impossible for any writer to not write on the Kumbha Mela after experiencing it. This book is my humble tribute to the Kumbha Mela, its sadhus, its *kalpavasis*, and its *tirthayatris*. I am humbled as I offer this book to the visitors of the 2025 Kumbha Mela at Prayaga.

Nityananda Misra
30 October 2018, Mumbai
Revised on 18 December 2024, Mumbai

Notes to the Reader

1) As I expect this book to be read by both laypersons and scholars, I follow a simple Roman transliteration scheme without diacritics for the most part in this book.

2) IAST (International Alphabet of Sanskrit Transliteration) diacritics and Devanagari are used ocassionally when discussing Sanskrit or Hindi words, roots, phrases, and verses. The citations in the appendix are in Devanagari.

3) For ease of readability and to save paper, there are no footnotes or endnotes in the book. The notes are planned to be published online shortly as a PDF under my Academia page (http://independent.academia.edu/MisraNityanand).

4) As is the convention in most parts of northern India, I follow the *purnimanta* mode of reckoning while referring to the months in the Hindu calendar.

5) By *Bhagavata Purana*, the *Srimadbhagavata Purana* (and not the *Devi Bhagavata Purana*) is meant.

6) In October 2018, the Uttar Pradesh government renamed the city of Prayagraj. The name Allahabad was changed to Prayagraj, a name popular among devout Hindus. In this book, I use the name Prayaga to refer to the area near the Sangama where the Kumbha Mela is held and the name Prayagraj for the city.

1. Introduction

The Sanskrit word *kumbha* (कुम्भ) refers to a pitcher or a jar of water. Another meaning of *kumbha* is the zodiac sign of Aquarius, specifically called *kumbha rashi*. The word *kumbha* has been used right since the Vedic times; it occurs in many Vedic verses. Another similar Vedic word is *kubha* which means "water", as in the word *kubhanyu* ("desirous of water") found in the Rig Veda. The word *kumbha* is derived from the root √*kubh* which means "to cover". That which covers something by water when being emptied is a *kumbha*. Alternatively, the word is derived as a compound of the word *ku* ("earth") with the word *umbha*, from the root √*umbh* ("to fill completely"). The *sandhi* (phonological combination) of the words *ku* and *umbha* should have resulted in the word *kūmbha* (कूम्भ) with the long vowel, but the irregular *sandhi* in case of *kumbha* (कुम्भ) can be explained by considering the word in the *shakandhvadi* group. Accordingly, *kumbha* means that which fills the earth [with water]. Finally, the word can also be derived by the *shakandhvadi sandhi* of the words *ka* ("water") and *umbha*. That which is filled completely with water or fills something completely with water is a *kumbha*.

The word *kumbha* has a sense of completeness. The Atharva Veda mentions a *purna kumbha* ("completely filled pitcher") placed above time (*kala*). Another word for *kumbha* in Sanskrit is *kalasha* (कलश), which literally means "that which achieves (makes) a pleasant sound [when being filled]". The *kumbha* or *kalasha* is traditionally worshipped by Hindus as a part of ritual deity worship (*puja*). A set of Sanskrit verses uttered during the worship of the *kalasha* are as follows (refer the appendix for the original verses):

"Vishnu rests at the mouth (top) of the *kalasha* and Shiva at its neck. Brahma is located at its base and *matrikas* (mother goddesses) at its middle portion. All the oceans and the earth with its seven islands are in its womb. The Rig Veda, the Yajur Veda, the Sama Veda, and the Atharva Veda all rest on the *kalasha* with their [six] limbs."

The word *mela* (मेला) is also a Sanskrit word. It comes from the root √*mil*, which has two meanings: "to unite or join" (*shleshana*) and "to move together" (*sangamana*). The Hindi verb *milna* (मिलना, "to meet" or "to be found") derives from this very Sanskrit root. In accordance with the two meanings of the root, *mela* in Sanskrit refers to both "an association or assembly" as well as "the act of moving together". The word *mela* reflects the spirit of *saṅgacchadhvam* ("move together") expressed in a verse (10.191.2) at the end of the Rig Veda:

"May you move together (be united in your actions). May you speak together (be united in your words). May your minds agree (may you be united in your thoughts). [May you all partake of everything together,] as the ancient deities are [ever] united and receive their [own] oblations."

Indeed, the Kumbha Mela is such a Hindu fair-cum-festival where Hinduism is seen in its completeness (signified by the word *kumbha*) and where all participants partake of piety and spirituality unopposed to each other in their actions, speech, and thought (signified by the word *mela*). True to its name, the Kumbha Mela is a celebration in complete unison.

Origin and History

The Kumbha Mela is held at an interval of twelve years (usually) at four places—Haridwar in Uttarakhand, Prayaga in Uttar Pradesh, Ujjain in Madhya Pradesh, and Nashik-Tryambakeshwar in Maharashtra. While some other Hindu festivals have also been called Kumbha Melas in the past and present, the term is most commonly used to refer to these four Kumbha Melas. It is difficult to say precisely when the tradition of these Kumbha Melas started. The traditional, historical, and astrological views on the topic are summarized in this section.

Traditional views

Many Hindus believe that the Kumbha Mela tradition exists from time immemorial. There are several verses in the Rig Veda, the Shukla Yajur Veda, and the Atharva Veda referring to the *kumbha* or *purna kumbha*. They are interpreted by some traditional scholars in the context of the Kumbha Melas. Specifically, a verse in the Atharva Veda (4.34.7 in Shaunakiya and 6.22.6 in Paippalada recension) refers to four *kumbhas*; this is interpreted by traditional scholars as being a reference to the four Kumbha Melas. Most modern scholars agree with the conclusion of Giorgio Bonazzoli who says, "such adaptations are recent and possibly restricted to small circles of adherents." It must, however, be pointed out that the Hindu tradition has been very open to new interpretations of Vedic verses. For example, a mystical verse in a hymn from the fourth book of the Rig Veda talks about a roaring bull with four horns, three feet, two heads, seven hands, and three tethers. The hymn is dedicated to five deities—Agni (fire), Surya (sun),

Jala (water), Go (speech), and Ghrita (ghee)—and the bull metaphor is accordingly interpreted in five ways. Patanjali in his *Mahabhashya* gave an entirely new interpretation of the bull as *Shabda Brahman*; the horns being parts of speech; the feet being the three tenses; the heads being the two types of words; the hands being the seven grammatical cases; and the tethers being the three places of articulation. It is possible that the tradition of designating the four melas as Kumbha Melas was started by pandits similarly giving a new interpretation of the inspiring Vedic verses mentioning the *kumbha*, the *purna kumbha*, and the four *kumbha*s. The Indian literary tradition has always welcomed new works and interpretations, as Kalidasa writes in the *Malavikagnimitra*: "Not everything is good just because it is old, and not every poetic work is inferior because it is new."

Some traditional accounts credit Adi Shankara, believed by many to have lived in the ninth century (the date is disputed), with starting the tradition of Kumbha Melas. However, there are no historical accounts to corroborate this belief. It is notable that Shaiva *akharas* have had a long history of participating in the Kumbha Melas and tradition credits Adi Shankara to be the founder of the *akharas* also.

As per another traditional belief, the four Kumbha Melas occur at the places where drops of *amrita* (nectar) fell from the pitcher of nectar (*amrita-kumbha*) that arose from the churning of the ocean. The following account is as per verses attributed to the *Skanda Purana*. These verses are not present in printed editions of the *Skanda Purana* and modern scholars doubt their authenticity. However, it is possible that the verses may have been a part of a lost manuscript or the oral literary tradition.

For the original Sanskrit verses, refer the appendix.

"Now I shall tell you the excellent account of the origin of the *kalasha*. In the North, near the Himalayas, there is the *kshirasagara* ocean. There the *devas* and the *danavas* started churning. They used the Mandara mountain as the churning-stick and the serpent Vasuki as the rope. They established Kurma at the base and the arms of Vishnu on the Mandara mountain. On one side were all the *devas* and on the other side were Bali and others (the *daityas*). Then, when the foremost ocean *kshirasagara* was churned, first the *Halahala* poison was produced which was consumed by Shiva. Then, the world was restored to its natural state (after Shiva consumed the poison). Now, those great *ratnas* (gems) that appeared will be described. First, the excellent Pushpaka Vimana, the best of all vehicles, appeared. Then the Airavata elephant and the Parijata tree appeared. The instrument veena was followed by the skilled danseuse Rambha. The best of jewels named Kaustubha and also the young moon appeared. Then earrings and the [Sharnga] bow, and five auspicious cows appeared. Next prosperity in the form of the good-natured Yamuna river and the Surabhi cow appeared. Then the Uchchaihsharavas horse appeared, followed by the fair-complexioned Lakshmi. Then the *deva* Dhanvantari, all-accomplishing and the knower of all arts, appeared. There appeared a *kalasha*, shining in Dhanvantari's hand. It was filled to the brim with nectar and stole everybody's heart. With the grace of the lotus-feet of the invincible lord (Vishnu) and impelled by the *devas*, the mighty and valorous Jayanta (Indra's son) saw the newly-arisen *kalasha* which was produced by the churning of the *kshirasagara* ocean and which was studded with divine gems.

He immediately took the nectar and went away. Shukra, the chief priest of the *daityas*, saw this act of the *devas* and informed the *daityas* who were made unconscious by the breaths of Vasuki. They (*daityas*) followed him closely and he (Jayanta) also fled, out of fear. He was continuously chased for ten days, day and night, in all ten directions. He was then held by the *daityas* and due to this, the *kalasha* was also taken from his hand. They (*devas* and *daityas*) raged against each other saying, 'I will drink it first, not you.' As the sons of Kashyapa (*devas* and *daityas*) were fighting thus over drinking nectar, the Lord beguiled them in the form of Mohini and then divided the nectar [among the *devas*]. During the fight of the sons of Kashyapa (*devas* and *daityas*), wherever the *kalasha* fell down on the earth, there the *Kumbha Parva* is said to occur. Guru (Jupiter), Chandra (Moon), Surya (Sun), and Shani (Saturn) protected the fallen *kalasha* from the *daityas*, whose minds were agitated by strife and who were impelled by Shukra. Chandra protected the *kalasha* from spilling nectar, Surya protected it from bursting, Guru protected it from the *daityas*, and Shani protected it from the fear of Jayanta [keeping all for himself]. When the combination of Sun, Moon, and Jupiter occurs in that constellation in a year, the ground [where the *kalasha* fell] is full of the *kumbha* of nectar and the *Kumbha Parva* occurs, not otherwise. Twelve *Kumbha Parva*s occur in twelve days of the *deva*s or twelve years of humans. For destroying the sins of humans, four take place on the earth in Bharata, the other eight are said to take place in another realm and are approachable by the *deva*s but not by others. A human who goes to the Kumbhas during the *yoga* (astronomical conjunction) becomes worthy of immortality. The *deva*s bow down to those present at the Kumbha as the poor bow down to the lords of wealth. On the earth, the *kumbha-yoga* is said to be of four types. At *Vishnudvara* (Haridwar), *Tirtharaja* (Prayaga), *Avanti* (Ujjain), and the banks of the Godavari (Nashik), the *Kumbha Parva* is well-known as the drops of nectar spilled there."

—Attributed to the *Skanda Purana*

Several Indian and non-Indian authors (including D. P. Dubey and Mark Tully) have mentioned that Jayanta took the form of a rook. This, however, is not mentioned in the verses attributed to the *Skanda Purana*.

Two other traditional accounts are also popular about the origin of the Kumbha Mela. As per the first, Garuda (the mount of Vishnu and the king of birds) was assigned the task of carrying the *amrita-kumbha* (pitcher of nectar) to the abode of Vishnu. While flying to Vishnu's abode, Garuda stopped at four places—Haridwar, Prayaga, Ujjain, and Nashik—putting down the *kumbha* on the earth for some time. As a result, these places became sacred and the tradition of the Kumbha Mela started. As per the second account, once Kadru enslaved Vinata, the mother of Garuda. To release Vinata from bondage, Garuda brought the *amrita-kumbha* from the *Nagaloka*. As he was flying to the ashram of his father Kashyapa, Indra attacked Garuda four times. The *amrita* from the *kumbha* spilled at the four places and the tradition of the Kumbha Mela started. Though both these accounts are popular, they do not find place in any of the extant versions of the Puranic texts.

Historical view

The Kumbha Mela of Haridwar, the annual Magha Mela of Prayaga (which is celebrated as the Kumbha Mela every twelve years), and the two Simhastha Melas of Ujjain and Nashik-Tryambakeshwar have been celebrated for many centuries and possibly even millennia. D. K. Roy states that the *Magha-snana* ("bathing during the *Magha* month") tradition dates to Neolithic times. Hsüan-tsang, who visited India in the seventh century, wrote about a fair that was held every five years at Prayaga in which King Harshavardhana participated. Some scholars interpret this to be a reference to the Ardha Kumbha (which is held five or six years after a Kumbha), but many other scholars conclude that the fair was not a Kumbha (Hsüan-tsang did not call it *kumbha* either). In the *Brahma Purana* (152.38–39), the river Gautami (Godavari) is said to be especially sacred as an embodiment of all *tirthas* (sacred places) when Guru (Jupiter) is *simhastha* or *simhasthita*, both meaning "situated in Leo". This is probably a reference to the Simhastha Mela tradition at Nashik. As per R. C. Hazra, the date of this chapter of the *Brahma Purana* is not known but Hazra believes that it is probably not older than the tenth century. Several Puranic texts (*Narada Purana*, *Padma Purana*, *Shiva Purana*, *Varaha Purana*, and *Brahma Purana*) mention the sacred months and/or astronomical combinations for bathing in the Ganga at Haridwar, in the Sangama at Prayaga, in the Shipra at Ujjain, and in the Godavari at Nashik. These months and/or astronomical combinations are the same as those for the current Magha and Kumbha Melas. This suggests that the melas were celebrated when the Puranas were composed, though they were most likely not called Kumbha Melas (with the possible exception of Haridwar, as would be clarified shortly). Several medieval works in India refer to the Kumbha, Simhastha, and Magha Melas. The *Gurucharitra* (c. late fifteenth century) of Sarasvati Gangadhara mentions the Simhastha Mela at Nashik. The *Ramacharitamanasa* (1574–76) of Tulasidasa refers to the annual Magha Mela at Prayaga. The *Bitaka* (1684) of Laladasa refers to the Kumbha Mela at Haridwar. Many written accounts of the Kumbha Mela in Haridwar and Prayaga are available from the nineteenth century onwards. The melas at Ujjain and Nashik, which have been called *Simhastha* for a long time, are now known as *Simhastha Kumbha Melas*. Since it is only at Haridwar among the four places that the Kumbha Mela is held when Jupiter is in Aquarius (*kumbha*), most modern authors and historians hold the view that the Haridwar Mela was known as the Kumbha Mela for a long time, and this name was adapted later for the other melas in the nineteenth and twentieth centuries.

Astrological view

Many scholars believe that the Kumbha Mela is named after the *kumbha* (Aquarius) astrological sign rather than the *amrita-kumbha* (pitcher of nectar) famous in Puranic accounts. As will be shown in the next chapter, the Haridwar Kumbha Mela is the only Mela where any of the celestial bodies which determine when the Mela is to be held is in Aquarius. Due to this, Subas Rai postulates that the Prayaga Kumbha may have been initially called the *Makara Kumbha Parva*, for the Sun is in Capricorn (*makara*) when the Mela is held. Swami Avadheshananda Giri of the Juna Akhara says that the Prayaga Kumbha is more precisely a *Makarastha Kumbha*. The Kumbha Melas at Ujjain and Nashik-Tryambakeshwar were earlier called *Simhastha Mela*s, as they are held when Jupiter is in Leo (*simha*), and are now called *Simhastha Kumbha Melas*. Even the

Kumbakonam fair (more on this later) is held when Jupiter is in Leo and can be called a *Simhastha [Kumbha] Mela*. Thus, from an astrological view also, it appears that the Haridwar Kumbha Mela was the original Mela and the name was adapted to extant melas at other places later. Swami Avadheshananda Giri is also of the view that the Haridwar Kumbha is the original Kumbha Mela or the *mula kumbha*.

Other Kumbha Melas

The popularity of the Kumbha Mela has led to several old and new similar gatherings in India being styled as Kumbha Melas. Multiple fairs in southern India have been likened to the Kumbha Mela. The nine-day festival called *Mahamaham* (also spelt *Mahamakham* and *Mahamagham*), held at Kumbakonam in Tamil Nadu once every twelve years, has been called the Kumbha Mela of the South for quite some time. It is simply referred to as Kumbha Mela in Kalyana's *Tirthanka* (1958) published by Gita Press. It was most recently held in February 2016 when an estimated forty lakh people visited Kumbakonam. The fair has much in common with the four Kumbha Melas—it is held every 12 years, its date is determined by the position of Jupiter, and it is associated with a legend around nectar spilling from a pitcher (*kumbha*). In addition, even the name Kumbakonam comes from Sanskrit 'Kumbhaghonam' (कुम्भघोणम्, "neck of the pitcher") as per a Sanskrit verse quoted in Kalyana's *Tirthanka*. Just like many *tirthayatris* from Uttar Pradesh and Bihar take pride in having attended multiple Kumbha Melas at Prayaga, several South Indians like Thanjai V. Gopalan (a retired public sector employee in Thanjavur) take pride in having attended many Mahamahams at Kumbakonam. Gopalan has attended all the six Kumbakonam Mahamahams that have been held since India's independence.

In 2015, the Godavari Maha Pushkaram was also called the Kumbha Mela of the South by a section of the media. Several crore people bathed at hundreds of ghats of the Godavari in multiple districts of Andhra Pradesh and Telangana over twelve days. While the number of participants was comparable to that of the four Kumbha Melas, the congregation spots were spread over a much larger area spanning multiple districts. In 2013, around 10,000 people participated in a Kumbha Mela held at the confluence of rivers Cauvery, Hemavathy, and Lakshman Theertha in Mandya, Karnataka.

The Rajim Kumbha is an annual fourteen-day festival held at the confluence of three rivers—the Mahanadi, the Pairi, and the Sondhur—at Rajim in Gariaband district of Chhattisgarh. Although recently started (it was held for the 13th time in 2018), it has grown quite popular in central India and saints like Jayendra Sarasvati (former Shankaracharya of Kanchi), Nishchalananda Sarasvati (Shankaracharya of Puri), and Sudhanshu Maharaja have attended it.

The Dashar Maha Kumbh was held at the confluence of the Sindhu and the Vitasta (Jhelum) in Ganderbal district of central Kashmir in June 2016. Hundreds of displaced Kashmiri Pandits participated in the Mela which was claimed to have been held after seventy-five years. The annual Ambubachi Mela, held near the Kamakhya Devi Mandir in Guwahati, has been called the Kumbha Mela of the North-East. It is attended by *tirtha-yatris*, Bauls, *aghoris*, sadhus, and foreigners.

In February 2018, the duodecennial *Mahamastakabhisheka* ritual of the colossal Bahubali statue at Shravanabelagola in Karnataka was organized. The event, attended by tens of lakhs of Jain devotees, was referred to as the Jain Maha Kumbha by several mainstream media publications.

Several large-scale non-religious festivals and fairs have also been called Kumbha Melas. In March 2016, the World Culture Festival organized by the Art of Living Foundation was called the "Kumbha Mela of culture" by the Indian Prime Minister. In November 2016, the Indian Council of Agricultural Research (ICAR) organized a *Krishi Kumbha* ("Kumbha for agriculture") which was attended by 10,000 farmers from seven states. Yet another festival called the *Samarasata Kumbha* ("Kumbha of the feeling of equality") has been planned in Ayodhya during December 2018.

Symbolism of the Kumbha Mela

Many Hindu practices have both a physical significance and a deeper metaphorical or spiritual significance. In the *Nirukta,* Yaska gives multiple meanings of many Vedic mantras calling them *adhiyajna* (relating to *yajna*), *adhidaivata* (relating to deities), or *adhyatma* (relating to *atman*). Several saints and writers have spoken or written about the spiritual significance (*adhyatma*) of the Kumbha Mela. As per Swami Satyamitrananda Giri, the Kumbha Mela symbolizes the refinement of human intellect (*buddhi*). He says that the shape of the human head is like that of a *kumbha* (earthen pot) and Supreme Atman (*paramatma*) is like a potter. The Kumbha Mela, as per the Swami, is the awakening of noble thoughts and feelings in the *kumbha* that is the human head. This is the internal journey or awakening that the Kumbha Mela represents in his view. A visit to the Kumbha Mela is thus meant to be both an internal and an external pilgrimage which take place simultaneously. To paraphrase Chidananda Muni, there is a quiet internal journey at the Kumbha Mela along with a boisterous external one.

D. P. Dubey writes that the Kumbha Mela's educative aspect is reflected in the significance of Jupiter in determining the time of its celebration, since Jupiter symbolizes learning and knowledge. In Sanskrit, Jupiter is known as *guru*, a word which also means a Vedic or spiritual teacher. In the Puranic texts, Jupiter is the guru of all deities and is also called *brihaspati* (बृह-स्पति) and *vachaspati* (वाचस्पति) in Sanskrit, both words meaning "the lord of Vedic verses". The external Kumbha is held when Jupiter is favourable (i.e., is in the right zodiac sign), and the internal journey of the Kumbha Mela occurs when the guru and learning become favourable.

As per S. L. Gupta, the number twelve, which is the duration in years between two Kumbha Melas, symbolizes the five *jnanendriyas* (organs of perception—the eyes, the ears, the nose, the tongue, and the skin), the five *karmendriyas* (organs of action—the hands, the feet, the larynx, the genitals, and the rectum), the mind, and the intellect. It is believed that the Kumbha Mela is attended by those who have mastered all twelve. Gupta adds that the four locations of the Kumbha Mela correspond to the four *purusharthas* ("goals of humans")—Haridwar to *dharma* (righteousness), Ujjain to *artha* (prosperity), Nashik to *kama* (desires), and finally Prayaga to *moksha* (liberation).

The following views of Purushottama Goswami on the significance of the Kumbha Mela have been documented by M. Darrol Bryant. As per Goswami, the Kumbha Mela is an opportunity for self-examination and meditation in addition to being a ritual of purification and renewal. The nectar of immortality that spilled on the locations of Kumbha Mela is nothing but *bhakti*, love of God or devotion to God. Through selfless devotion, humans attain God and immortality. Therefore, the purpose of the Kumbha Mela is to solely focus on *bhakti* towards God. The heart is the pot (*kumbha*) which needs to be empty of arrogance and pride.

Finally, the *triveni sangama* at Prayaga where the largest Kumbha Mela is held also has a deeper meaning. In the *Ramacharitamanasa*, Tulasidasa presents a lovely metaphor. He says that the assembly of saints is like a moving Prayaga, where the *bhakti* of Rama is the Ganga, the *katha* (discourse) on *karma* consisting of injunctions and prohibitions is the Yamuna, and the propagation of the contemplation of Brahman, i.e. *jnana*, is the Sarasvati. The Sangama at Prayaga thus represents a confluence of *bhakti*, *karma*, and *jnana* in the spiritual realm. J. L. Mehta notes that the Ganga represents the central Vedic strand, the Yamuna represents the mystical *bhakti* strand of the Vedic Soma-vision, and the Sarasvati represents the strand of language-born knowledge. It is to be noted that Sarasvati is the goddess of speech and knowledge in Hinduism.

Tradition and Modernity

The Kumbha Mela is not only a comprehensive meeting platform for people, communities, and thoughts, it is also a platform where tradition and modernity combine in perfect harmony to create an enriching experience for everybody. The number of people visiting the Mela has increased tremendously over the past few decades, despite the fact that the average Hindu *tirthayatri* visiting the Mela today is more affluent and more literate compared to the one several decades ago. This would not have been possible without either the belief tradition or technological modernity. At the Kumbha Mela, both tradition and modernity move together, following the spirit of the *saṅgacchadhvam* mantra, and enrich each other. The *akhara*s of sadhus and religious organizations work hand in hand with the Mela Administration which uses the latest technology to provide the infrastructure, the transport services, the food and water supplies, the medical facilities, the electricity, the security, and above all the human touch required to successfully conduct the largest mass gathering on earth. This is how scientific and technological modernity helps the faith tradition. In turn, it is a strong traditional belief which brings millions of *tirthayatris* to the Kumbha Mela and this provides an immense learning opportunity for multi-disciplinary studies in the fields of urban planning, commerce, business, religious studies, public health, governance, and mass gathering event management. It is this marriage of tradition and modernity which makes the Kumbha Mela a unique event which is traditionally modern in many senses. In this book, I touch on all three aspects—the tradition of the Kumbha Mela, the modernity of the Kumbha Mela, and how the interaction of tradition and modernity in the twenty-first century makes the Kumbha Mela *traditionally modern*.

The rest of the book is structured as follows. The second chapter discusses the venues and dates of the four Kumbha Melas. The organization of the Kumbha Mela, a wonder of modern management, is dealt with in the third chapter. The fourth chapter takes the reader on a quick tour through the world of sadhus at the Kumbha Mela. The other traditional participants in the Mela, *kalpavasis* and *tirthayatris*, are covered in the fifth chapter. In the sixth chapter, I show how some new-age Hindu movements have added to the experience of the Kumbha Mela with their participation. The triple confluence of literature, arts, and music at the Kumbha Mela is described in the seventh chapter. The eighth chapter delves into the confluence of tradition with modern commerce and technology at the Kumbha Mela. The diversity and inclusivity of the Mela, which I believe is not emphasized enough, is covered in the ninth chapter. The tenth chapter shows how the Kumbha Mela is not just a celebration of the nectar of immortality, but it is also an immortal Mela itself. In the eleventh chapter, I describe my personal experiences from the four Kumbha Melas I have been to. Finally, a summary of the upcoming 2025 Kumbha at Prayaga is provided in the last chapter. A consistent theme that comes across all chapters is that of diverse people, communities, and organizations coming together and working together at the Kumbha Mela, something I refer to as the *saṅgacchadhvam* spirit of the Kumbha Mela.

2. Venues and Dates

The Kumbha Mela is held at Haridwar on the banks of the Ganga near Har Ki Pauri; at Prayaga near the triple confluence (*triveni sangama*) of the Ganga, the Yamuna, and the invisible Sarasvati; at Ujjain on the banks of the Shipra near Rama Ghat; and at Nashik-Tryambakeshwar on the banks of the Godavari near Rama Kunda and Kushavarta Kunda. The Mela is organized when a specific astronomical combination (*kumbha yoga*) of the Moon, the Sun, and Jupiter occurs in specific zodiac signs. The Moon takes around one month (27.32 days) to orbit the earth during which it transits through the 12 signs. The Sun transits through the 12 signs in around one year (365.2425 days), the time taken by the earth to orbit the Sun. Finally, Jupiter transits through the 12 signs in nearly 12 years (11.8618 years), the time taken by it to orbit the Sun. The transit period of Jupiter being the longest—12 times that of the Sun and around 159 times that of the moon—the *kumbha yoga* for a location repeats when Jupiter enters the same sign again. This is why the Kumbha Mela is held once every 12 years at a given venue, as a general rule.

The seventh Mela after six melas held in 72 years (each held 12 years after the previous one) is held 11 years after the sixth Mela, giving us seven melas in 83 years. The reason is that Jupiter completes seven transits of the zodiac in nearly 83 years ($11.8618 \times 7 = 83.0326$), and moves to the next sign in the 84th year. This is why the Haridwar Kumbha was held in 1938 after 1927 and the Prayaga Kumbha was held in 1977 after 1966. In Haridwar, after 2010 (1938 + 72), the next Kumbha was held in 2021 (1938 + 83 = 2010 + 11).

While 12 years is an overestimate for the time taken by Jupiter to transit through the 12 zodiac signs once, 83 years is an underestimate for seven such transits. Fortunately, 83.0326 is very close to 83, so the thumb rule of seven Kumbha Melas in 83 years works well for a reasonably long period of time. Using the logic used to add leap days to a year, it is easy to see that one year will need to be added every 2490 years to bring the Mela cycle in sync with Jupiter's position. In other words, after 29 cycles of seven Kumbha Melas in 83 years, the next seven Kumbha Melas are to be held in 84 years. This gives us 210 Kumbha Melas in 2,491 (29 × 83 + 84) years. The time taken by Jupiter to complete 210 transits of the zodiac is nearly 2,491 years (11.8618 × 210 = 2490.978).

These thumb rules (1 in 12, 7 in 83, and 210 in 2,491) do not always work since the apparent movement of Jupiter across the zodiac signs neither has uniform speed nor is always direct. On average, Jupiter stays for around one year in a sign, but sometimes this period is much shorter. For example, as per the Western (*sayana*) mode of reckoning, Jupiter entered Aries on 21 December 2022 and then Taurus on 17 May 2023, staying in Aries for only 147 days. Similarly, as per the traditional Indian (*nirayana*) mode of reckoning, Jupiter entered *dhanus* (Sagittarius) on 5 November 2019 and then *makara* (Capricorn) on 30 March 2020, staying in *dhanus* for 147 days. The position of a heavenly body as per *nirayana* reckoning, used for holding the Kumbha Mela, is obtained by subtracting the *ayanamsha* (currently around 24 degrees) from the *sayana* position.

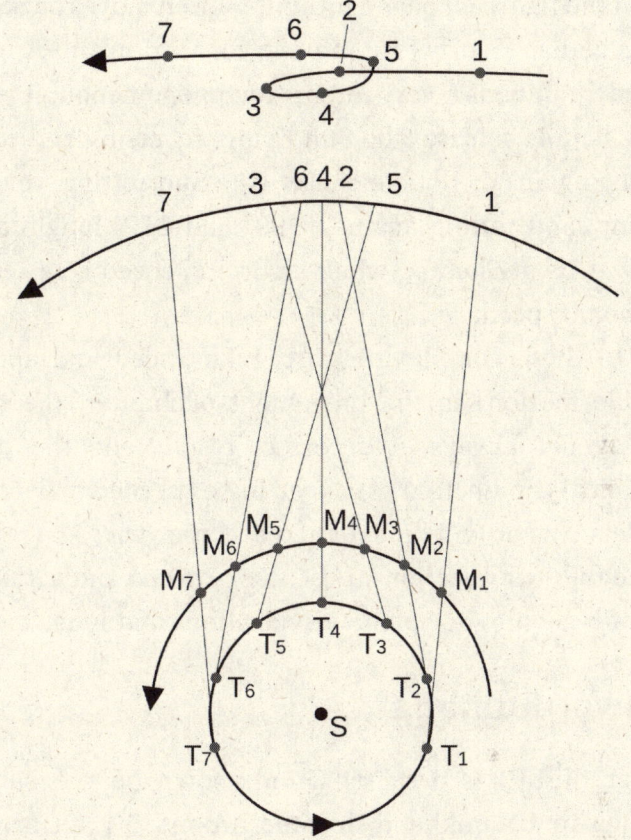

Retrograde motion of planet M as seen from planet T.
Source: Illustration from Wikimedia Commons.

The non-uniform movement of Jupiter across the signs is even further complicated by what is called apparent retrograde motion. The Earth overtakes Jupiter in their motion around the Sun once every 399 days (synodic period). When this happens, Jupiter appears (*apparent*) to move backwards (*retrograde*) for some months before moving forward again (direct motion). Due to this apparent retrograde motion (*vakra-gati* in Sanskrit), shown in the figure on page 19, Jupiter often moves back to the previous zodiac sign before moving forward again. Apparent retrograde motion is a very interesting phenomenon; it is what causes a double sunrise (the Sun rising, reversing and setting, and rising again) or double sunset (the Sun setting, reversing and rising, and setting again) at 90° and 270° longitudes on Mercury at its perihelion, when its orbital speed is faster than its rotational speed.

Due to these complexities (irregular speed and apparent retrograde motion) in the movement of Jupiter, the thumb rules may not always give correct results and the precise astronomical conjunction may need to be checked to determine if the Mela was or will be held in a specific year.

In the following sections, I use the *nirayana* and *purnimanta* modes of reckoning for planetary positions and lunar months.

Haridwar Kumbha

Haridwar (हरिद्वार) is a sacred Hindu town on the banks of the Ganga in Uttarakhand, located around 50 km from the capital Dehradun and 35 km from the Jolly Grant Airport. It is served by the Haridwar Junction, a railway station under the Northern Railway zone. As per the 2011 census, the town had a population of 3 lakh and a literacy rate of 85.43%.

Haridwar is also called Hardwar (हरद्वार). The former name means "the door or gate of Hari (Vishnu)" while the latter means "the door or gate of Hara (Shiva)". As the two names indicate, the town is held sacred by both Vaishnavas and Shaivas. Coincidentally, both Vishnu's name *Hari* and Shiva's name *Hara* come from the same root √*hr* and mean the same, "he who removes [sins] or takes [sins] away". The main venue of the Mela at Haridwar is the Har Ki Pauri (हर की पौड़ी, "Shiva's steps") which is, not surprisingly, also called Hari Ki Pauri (हरि की पौड़ी, "Vishnu's steps").

The Kumbha Mela is held in Haridwar on the banks of the Ganga when Jupiter is in Aquarius and the Sun is in Aries. As a popular verse (see the appendix) attributed to the *Skanda Purana* goes:

"When the lord of lotuses (the Sun) is in Aries and Jupiter has entered Aquarius, then the excellent *yoga* (combination) named *kumbha* occurs at the gateway to Ganga (Haridwar)."

Although the Sun enters Aries in April, the Haridwar Kumbha in current times is held from January to April, as was the case with the 2010 Purna Kumbha and the 2016 Ardha Kumbha. The 2010 Haridwar Kumbha had three royal bath (*shahi snana*) days:

1) *Maha Shivaratri* on 12 February. *Maha Shivaratri* falls in either February or March on the fourteenth day of the dark half (*krishna paksha*) of the *Phalguna* lunar month.

2) *Chaitra Amavasya* on 15 March. The new moon day of the *Chaitra* month falls around one month after *Maha Shivaratri*.

3) *Mesha Sankranti* (also known as *Baisakhi*) on 14 April. This is the day when the Sun enters Aries (as per the *nirayana* mode of reckoning).

In all, there were eleven *snana* days at the 2010 Purna Kumbha and ten at the 2016 Ardha Kumbha. More than 5 crore people visited the 2010 Haridwar Kumbha, with around 1.5 crore present on the 14 April *shahi snana* day. These numbers were up from 1 crore and 46 lakh in the 1998 Kumbha, and 55 lakh and 26 lakh in the 1992 Ardha Kumbha. In 1986, around

70 lakh people had visited the Haridwar Kumbha. In 24 years from 1986 to 2010, there was nearly a seven-fold increase in the number of people visiting the Haridwar Kumbha. Over the same time, India's population grew by around 54% and her literacy rate grew from under 50% to nearly 75%.

In 2021, the low-key Haridwar Kumbha drew far fewer visitors due to the COVID-19 pandemic: around 90 lakh people attended the Mela. The Mela was held for only a month and was cut short on the appeal of the Prime Minister following the outbreak of the second wave of the pandemic in India.

Prayaga Kumbha

Prayaga (प्रयाग) or Prayagraj (प्रयागराज) is located in southern Uttar Pradesh, at a distance of 130 km from Varanasi. It is served by Bamrauli Airport, which is being upgraded as part of the preparations of the 2025 Kumbha. The city has seven railway stations under the Northern, North Eastern, and North Central zones. As per the 2011 census, the city had a population of 12 lakh and a literacy rate of 86.06%.

Prayaga is considered the most sacred of all holy sites by Hindus. For this reason, it is known as *tirtharaja* (तीर्थराज, "the king of sacred places"). The word *prayaga* is derived from the root √*yaj* which has three meanings—worshipping a deity by a *yajna* (*deva-puja*), coming together (*sangati-karana*), and donating (*dana*). The word *yaga* (याग) from this root means an act of worshipping (i.e. a *yajna*), coming together, or donating. The place where there is an eminent *yaga* is called *prayaga*. It is believed that Brahma performed a great *yajna* at Prayaga. From the meaning "coming together", a confluence of rivers is also called *prayaga* as in the *Pancha Prayagas*, the five confluences in the Himalayas (Vishnuprayaga, Nandaprayaga, Karnaprayaga, Rudraprayaga, and Devaprayaga). At Prayaga, there is the confluence (*sangama*) of the Ganga, the Yamuna, and the invisible (*guptasalila*) Sarasvati. Finally, charity (donation) at a *tirtha* like Prayaga is especially eulogized. Thus, Prayaga is the place of all three—an eminent *yajna*, an eminent confluence, and eminent donations. The name *prayagaraja* is alluded to in a verse from the *Brahma Purana*, as cited in the *Tristhalisetu*—"It is *prayaga* due to its eminence and it has the sound (i.e. is suffixed with) *raja* (meaning 'a king') due to its supremacy."

A beautiful metaphor of Prayaga as a king is presented by Tulasidasa in the *Ramacharitamanasa*. He says of King Prayaga (see the appendix for the original verses), "Truth (*satya*) is his minister, devotion (*shraddha*) is his dear wife, and [the twelve] Madhavas are his beneficial friends. His storehouse is replete with the four entities (*dharma*, *artha*, *kama*, and *moksha*). The sacred land [of Prayaga] is his extremely beautiful dominion. The region [near Sangama] shines forth as the impenetrable and strong fort which cannot be breached by the enemies (sins) even in their dreams. All the sacred sites are the brave warriors of his army, they are skilled in battle and destroy many vices. The Sangama is his exquisite royal throne. The *Akshaya Vata*, which charms the minds of even the sages, is his royal umbrella. The waves of the Yamuna and the Ganga are his *chowries*. Just on seeing him, sorrows and desires are destroyed. Virtuous and pious sadhus wait upon him and attain all that their mind desires. The Vedas and Puranas are the court singers who narrate his immaculate virtues."

The Kumbha Mela is held at Prayaga when Jupiter is in Taurus and the Sun is in Capricorn. A popular Sanskrit verse (see the appendix) of untraceable origin goes:

"When the lord of the days (the Sun) is in Capricorn and Jupiter is in Taurus, the extremely rare *kumbha yoga* occurs in Prayaga."

The Prayaga Kumbha lasts around two months, starting on *Makara Sankranti* (14 January) and ending on *Maha Shivaratri* in February or March. The dates of the three royal baths are:

1) *Makara Sankranti* (14 January), when the Sun enters Capricorn (as per *nirayana* reckoning).

2) *Mauni Amavasya*, the new moon day of the *Magha* month which falls in late January or February. The word *mauni* (मौनी) means "silent". It comes from the word *mauna* (मौन) ("silence") which in turn is derived from the word *muni* (मुनि) ("a sage"). Silence is one of the attributes of a *muni*. Many *tirthayatris* take up a vow of silence on this day.

3) *Vasanta Panchami*, the fifth day of the bright half (*shukla paksha*) of the *Magha* month.

In all, there were nine *snana* days at the 2013 Prayaga Kumbha which was visited by around 12 crore people. Despite being an Ardha Kumbha, the 2019 Mela saw twice as many visitors: around 24 crore people. An estimated three crore people took a dip in the Sangama on *Mauni Amavasya*, the biggest bathing day, in 2013. In the 2019 Ardha Kumbha, this number went up to five crore. An estimated 60 lakh people had visited the Sangama on the *Mauni Amavasya* day in 1954 (3 February), the day when a stampede killed hundreds. As early as in 1977, the number of people bathing at the Prayaga Kumbha on *Mauni Amavasya* had crossed one crore.

The growing numbers of *tirthayatris* at the Prayaga Kumbha have been mentioned in the Preface.

Ujjain Kumbha

Ujjain, from Sanskrit *ujjayini* (उज्जयिनी) which means "she who is victorious", is a sacred town located in western Madhya Pradesh, around 60 km from Indore's Devi Ahilya Bai Holkar Airport. Ujjain has five railway stations which come under the Western Railway zone. As per the 2011 Census, Ujjain had a population of 5 lakh and a literacy rate of 85.55%. The town is famous for the Mahakaleshvara Mandir which houses the Mahakala Jyotirlinga, believed to be one of the twelve effulgent emblems of Shiva.

The Kumbha Mela is held in Ujjain on the banks of the Shipra when the Sun is in Aries and Jupiter is in Leo. When in Leo (*simha*), a planet is said to be *simhastha* (सिंहस्थ). As Jupiter is *simhastha* when the Ujjain Kumbha is held, it is also known as *Simhastha Kumbha*. A popular Sanskrit verse (refer the appendix) goes:

"When the Sun has entered Aries and Jupiter is in Leo, the *kumbha* [*yoga*] occurs in Ujjayini (Ujjain). It is always the bestower of liberation."

The Ujjain Kumbha is the shortest among all four Kumbha Melas, lasting for one month. It is held over April and May, two of the hottest months in Ujjain and India. At the 2016 Ujjain Kumbha, the three dates of royal bath were:

1) *Chaitra Purnima* on 22 April, the full moon day of the *Chaitra* month and the first day of the Mela.

2) *Akshaya Tritiya* on 9 May, the third day of the bright half

(*shukla paksha*) of the *Vaishakha* month.

3) *Vaishakha Purnima* on 21 May, the full moon day of the *Vaishakha* month and the last day of the Mela.

An estimated five to six crore people visited Ujjain during the 2016 Kumbha. This was more than two times the number during the 2004 Kumbha (2–3 crore) and five to six times that during the 1992 Kumbha (one crore).

Nashik-Tryambakeshwar Kumbha

Nashik, a holy city for Vaishnavas, is a located at a distance of around 185 km from Mumbai in north-west Maharashtra. It had a population of more than 15 lakh and a literacy rate of 90.97% as per the 2011 Census. The closest airport to Nashik is in Mumbai. The city is served by the Nasik Road railway station which comes under the Central Railway zone.

While the city is known as *Nashik* (नाशिक) in Marathi, it is called *Nasik* (नासिक) in other major Indian languages including Hindi, Telugu, Kannada, Gujarati, etc. The name of the city is believed to have come from Sanskrit word *nasika* (नासिका), which means "the nose". Another possibility is that the name comes from *nasikya* (नासिक्य), a Sanskrit word for a geographical region around Nashik which literally means "[coming from] the nose". It is believed that Lakshmana had cut off the nose of Shurpanakha at this place when she tried to kill Sita as per the Ramayana of Valmiki.

Tryambakeshwar or Trimbak is a Shaiva pilgrimage place located at a distance of 30 km from Nashik. Its name comes from the temple which houses the Tryambakeshvara (त्र्यम्बकेश्वर) Jyotirlinga, one of the twelve effulgent symbols of Shiva.

The word *tryambaka* (त्र्यम्बक), a name of Shiva, famously occurs in *Maha Mrityunjaya Mantra*. According to the *Vyakhya Sudha* commentary on the *Amara Kosha*, the word has eight meanings—(1) one who has three eyes; (2) one who has his sight on the three [worlds]; (3) the father of the three worlds; (4) one who sounds (speaks) the three Vedas; (5) one whose word (the Vedas) are present in the three worlds; (6) one whose word (the Vedas) are present in all the three times (past, present, and future); (7) one who has three sounds as his appellation: *a*, *u*, and *m* (which together make up the sound OM); and (8) one who has three mothers—the *svarga* (heaven), the earth, and the waters. Finally, one who is *tryambaka* and also *ishvara* ("the Lord") is *tryambakeshvara*, i.e. Shiva.

The Kumbha Mela is held on the banks of the Godavari when both the Sun and Jupiter are in Leo (*simhastha*). For this reason, the Nashik-Tryambakeshwar Kumbha is also known as Simhastha Kumbha. As a popular Sanskrit verse (refer the appendix) goes:

"When the Sun has entered Leo and Jupiter is [also] in Leo, the *kumbha* [*yoga*]—which bestows devotion and liberation—occurs on the banks of the Godavari."

The Nashik-Tryambakeshwar Kumbha lasts for around two months, from July or August to September. The three days for the royal bath at the 2015 Kumbha were:

1) *Shravana Purnima* on 29 August, the full moon day of the *Shravana* month which is celebrated as *Raksha Bandhan*.

2) *Bhadrapada Amavasya* on 13 September, the new moon day of the *Bhadrapada* month.

3) *Rishi Panchami* on 18 September in Nashik (for Vaishnava *akharas*) and *Vamana Dvadashi* on 25 September

in Tryambakeshwar (for Shaiva *akharas*). *Rishi Panchami* and *Vamana Dvadashi* fall on the fifth and twelfth days, respectively, of the bright half of *Bhadrapada*.

Several crore people (estimates vary) attended the 2015 Nashik-Tryambakeshwar Kumbha. On an average, the three *shahi snana* days saw 80 lakh to 1 crore people in Nashik and 25 to 30 lakh in Tryambakeshwar. The number of *tirthayatris* was several times the number (50 lakh as per some estimates) during the 2003 Kumbha. The *akharas' dharma-dhvajas* ("flags of *dharma*"), which were raised on 29 June 2015, were not lowered for more than a year till 11 August 2016. The lowering of the flags at Nashik and Tryambakeshwar marked the official close of the Simhastha Kumbha, though most sadhus, saints, and *tirthayatris* had already left the Mela area many months ago (in September 2015).

The doors of the Ganga Godavari Mandir near Rama Kunda at Nashik are opened only when the Kumbha Mela is in progress. The temple was open for the last time from 14 July 2015 to 12 August 2016. It will next open in the year 2027.

Ardha Kumbha

The Ardha Kumbha ("half Kumbha") Mela is held at Haridwar and Prayaga six years after the Kumbha Mela, halfway between two Kumbhas. This tradition is based on a verse (refer the appendix) attributed to the *Shakti-yamala Tantra* which goes:

"The Ardha Kumbha is the half-fruit which is to be known at the time of half year after five-and-a-half years from the Kumbha. It bestows liberation."

As per the traditional nomenclature, the last Ardha Kumbha

at Prayaga was held in 2019 and the one at Haridwar was held in 2016. To distinguish it from the Ardha Kumbha, the regular Kumbha Mela is often called the Purna Kumbha ("full Kumbha"). However, in a clever marketing move, the 2019 Ardha Kumbha was marketed as Kumbha by the authorities and the 2025 Purna Kumbha is similarly being marketed as a Maha Kumbha.

While the Ardha Kumbha does not draw as many sadhus and *tirthayatris* as the Purna Kumbha, the numbers are still quite high. As per a BBC report, around 2 crore people bathed at the Sangama on *Mauni Amavasya* at the 2007 Ardha Kumbha in Prayaga. This was two-thirds of the number of people who bathed on *Mauni Amavasya* at the 2013 Purna Kumbha in Prayaga. In the 2019 Ardha Kumbha, the number was five crore, as mentioned previously.

The Ardha Kumbha is not held at Nashik-Tryambakeshwar and Ujjain, though some attempts have been made in the past to organize it at Ujjain. Sandhyapuri Maharaja of the Datta Akhara observed an Ardha Kumbha at Ujjain in 1950 by bathing with sadhus and saints and holding a *Maharudrayajna*. In 1986, Pandit Anandashankar Vyas made attempts to organize an Ardha Kumbha at Ujjain, but it did not get popular support.

The Kumbha Mela held in 2019 at Prayaga was an Ardha Kumbha as per the traditional definition. The Uttar Pradesh government decided to brand it as a Kumbha and the 2025 Purna Kumbha as a Maha Kumbha. It remains to be seen if the sadhus, saints, and *tirthayatris*—to whom the Mela rightfully belongs—agree with this decision of the Uttar Pradesh government or if they continue using the traditional nomenclature of Ardha Kumbha and Purna Kumbha.

Disagreements in Dates

Sometimes, there arises a difference of opinion among astrologers on when to hold the Kumbha Mela. Such a situation arose regarding the Prayaga Kumbha in 1965 and 1966. On 14 January 1965, Jupiter was in Aries (22°45' with the Lahiri Ayanamsha) when the Sun entered Capricorn. The next year, on 14 January 1966, Jupiter was in Taurus (29°33' with the Lahiri Ayanamsha) when the Sun entered Capricorn. If one goes by just these calculations, the Kumbha should have been held in 1966. However, Shaiva and Vaishnava astrologers differed on when the Kumbha should be held, and as a result the crowds were split in 1965 and 1966. The Uttar Pradesh government made arrangements in both years. There was no such disagreement for the next Mela and it was organized only in 1977. Jupiter was in Aries on 14 January 1977 (27°38' with the Lahiri Ayanamsha) and had moved to Gemini in the next year on 14 January 1978 (4°42' with the Lahiri Ayanamsha).

Relation between Kumbhas

We have seen before that Jupiter stays for almost one year on average in a zodiac sign. The Haridwar Kumbha Mela is held when Jupiter is in Aquarius while the Prayaga Kumbha is held when it is in Taurus, which is the third sign from Aquarius. It is clear then that the Prayaga Kumbha Mela should occur almost three years after the Haridwar Kumbha Mela. This is generally true: the Kumbha Melas at Haridwar in 1974, 1986, 1998, and 2010 were followed three years later by those at Prayaga in

1977, 1989, 2001, and 2013 respectively. Due to the irregular movement of Jupiter, the Prayaga Kumbha is sometimes held four years after the Haridwar Kumbha. For example, the 2021 Haridwar Kumbha is being followed by the Prayaga Kumbha in 2025.

The Ujjain and Nashik-Tryambakeshwar Kumbha Melas are both held when Jupiter is in Leo. In case of the former, the Sun is in Aries and in case of the latter, it is in Leo. Leo is the fourth sign from Aries, and Aries is the eighth sign from Leo. As a result, the two melas are held within four or eight months of each other. They are held either in the same Gregorian year with the Ujjain Kumbha in April–May followed by the Nashik-Tryambakeshwar Kumbha in August–September (as happened in 1968, 1980, and 1992), or in successive Gregorian years with the Nashik-Tryambakeshwar Kumbha in August–September followed by the Ujjain Kumbha in April–May next year (as happened in 2003 and 2004, and 2015 and 2016). Despite the two melas being held in quick succession, many sadhus and saints attend both.

The Mahamaham at Kumbakonam, often called the Kumbha Mela of the South, is also held when Jupiter is in Leo. For the past eight times (1933, 1945, 1957, 1968, 1980, 1992, 2004, and 2016), it has been held in the same Gregorian year as the Ujjain Kumbha.

It is commonly said that the four Kumbha Melas are held at intervals of three years, but this is not true. All the four Kumbha Melas are normally held within a span of six or seven years, and then there is no Purna Kumbha for the next five to six years.

The Haridwar Ardha Kumbha Mela often falls in the same Gregorian year as the Ujjain and the Nashik-Tryambakeshwar

Kumbha Mela, as happened in 1968, 1980, and 1992. At other times, the Haridwar Ardha Kumbh and the Ujjain Kumbha are held in the same Gregorian year.

3. Organization

If there is anything more jaw-dropping than the scale of the Kumbha Mela, it is the planning and organization that goes behind making the event a success. The number of government departments and ministries involved in the organization is astonishing—for the 2025 Kumbha, 15 state government departments have implemented more than 500 projects. For the first time, the state government and the central government are jointly hosting the Mela. Usually the experience of working with one government department is enough to experience the inefficiencies in Indian bureaucracy. However, when it comes to the Kumbha Mela, somehow the authorities pull off the achievement of efficient organization of the Kumbha Mela every single time. An example of this achievement against all odds is given by Mark Tully from his experience of the 1989 Prayaga Kumbha. In 1988, the monsoon was heavy and the river bed had not dried till late October. Various government departments had to work on a war footing to set up the *Kumbha Nagari* before January. Tully wrote that this was "one war the Indian bureaucracy did win" and that the spectacle was "a triumph for the much-maligned Indian administration". Great planning and effort are required for the organization of the Kumbha Melas, especially the Prayaga Kumbha where an ephemeral megacity is built and dismantled within a span of just a few months on an area which remains under water during the monsoon.

Many aspects of planning and organization are common across the four Kumbha Melas—development and upgradation of infrastructure (airports, roads, bridges, flyovers, parking lots, ghats), allocating space to organizations, travel and transportation arrangements (running buses and special trains), provision of basic necessities (food, water, and fuel supplies), electrification, sanitation, setting up lost and found centres, security of the Mela (policing and monitoring crowds), disaster response, provision of medical services, information and public relations (website, helpdesks), etc. In addition, there are some preparations which are specific to each Kumbha Mela. For example, lakhs of *kalpavasis* (see chapter 5) are present at the Prayaga Kumbha Mela and special arrangements have to be made for their camps. Sometimes unforeseen situations arise for only one year at a Kumbha Mela. As an example, the Ganga flowed in two streams during the 1977 Prayaga Kumbha and joined the Yamuna at two places, creating two Sangama-s where the *tirthayatris* bathed.

The Kumbha Nagari

The area over which the Kumbha Mela is held is called the *Kumbha Nagara* or *Kumbha Nagari* ("the Kumbha city"). The size of the Kumbha Nagari varies across the four venues and even across two Kumbha Melas at the same venue.

Haridwar

Like in 2010, most of the Mela activities at the 2021 Haridwar Kumbha were held over a 20 sq km area. A much larger area (156 sq km) comprising parts of Dehradun, Pauri Garhwal, and Haridwar regions was notified as Mela area. The area was divided into 41 sectors, nine more than those in the 2010 Kumbha. Preparations for setting up the Kumbha Nagari started a few months before the beginning of the Mela, though the planning had started much earlier. The main venue of the Kumbha Mela at Haridwar is the Har Ki Pauri where there is permanent construction.

Prayaga

The Kumbha Nagari at Prayaga is unique as more than 80% of the area under the temporary city is under water during the monsoon season. It is exposed only when the water recedes after the monsoon. When not being prepared or used for the Mela, the exposed area is sometimes used for agriculture. Any work on the sandy area can start only after the exposed river bed has dried, which leaves only eight weeks before the first inhabitants arrive for the Magha Mela or the Kumbha Mela. Tractors are used to flatten the mud and sand on the river bed to form a flat foundation of the Kumbha Nagari, and embankments are made to prevent the Ganga from changing course. At the 2013 Kumbha, the Kumbha Nagari was spread over an area of 20 sq km which was divided into fourteen sectors. At the 2019 Ardha Kumbha, the Kumbha Nagari had an area of 32 sq km divided into twenty sectors. In the upcoming 2025 Kumbha, the Kumbha Nagari will have an area of 40 sq km divided into twenty-five sectors. The Kumbha Nagari in Prayaga is a fully-functional metropolis which is assembled from scratch, inhabited, and dismantled completely—all in a short span of five months. In 2013, the city had its own banks (nationalized banks operated out of plywood offices), courthouse (offences committed in the Mela were heard in a canvas tent), and administration (including a district collector, a police superintendent, and a chief medical officer). As per M. P. Mishra, Mela Adhikari in 2013, the Kumbha Nagari was the largest city in the world in terms of population density, but the only catch was that the city does not really exist in a permanent sense.

Ujjain

The Kumbha Nagari at the 2016 Ujjain Kumbha was spread over an area of more than 30 sq km and was divided into six zones—Mahakala Zone, Datta Akhara Zone, Mangalanatha Zone, Kala Bhairava Zone, Triveni Zone, and Chamunda Mata Zone. The zones were further divided into 22 sectors which hosted temporary townships. Plots in the Datta Akhara Zone were allotted to Shaiva organizations, as Shaiva *akharas* traditionally bathe at the Datta Akhara Ghat during the Ujjain Kumbha. Plots in the Mangalanatha Zone were allotted to Vaishnava, Udasina, and Sikh organizations as their *akharas* traditionally bathe at Rama Ghat during the Ujjain Kumbha.

Nashik-Tryambakeshwar

A unique feature of the Nashik-Tryambakeshwar Kumbha Mela is that the Shaiva and Vaishnava *akharas* have their royal bath (*shahi snana*) at two different places in two different cities, separated by around 30 km. Sadhus of the Shaiva *akharas* bathe at the Kushavarta Kunda in Trimbak, the Shaiva holy city of the Tryambakeshvara Jyotirlinga Mandira. Sadhus of Vaishnava *akharas* bathe at the Rama Kunda in Panchavati, the Vaishnava holy city in the north of Nashik which is believed to be the place where Rama, Lakshmana, and Sita stayed during their exile. When Shaiva and Vaishnava *akhara*s quarrelled over the *shahi snana* in the late eighteenth century, Peshwa Madhav Rao II made them agree to the current arrangement.

At Nashik and Tryambakeshwar, special areas called *sadhugramas* ("villages for sadhus") were set up for the first time during the 2003 Kumbha. The *sadhugrama* at Trimbak was spread over 15 acres and had 80 plots. A much larger *sadhugrama* was set up at Tapovan in Nashik with 250 plots. In 2015, the *sadhugrama* was spread over 300 acres at Tapovan and had 1,729 plots with a total plot area of more than 6 lakh sq metres. It was divided into four zones and hosted around three lakh Vaishnava sadhus during the Mela.

Roads, Bridges, and Ghats

The Kumbha Mela requires development and upgradation of infrastructure to handle the flow of crores of visitors. This includes the construction of new roads and flyovers, laying of temporary bridges, creation of bathing ghats, and sometimes construction of buildings too. All this leads to improvement in the infrastructure of the venue hosting the Kumbha Mela. In 2003, all major existing roads in Nashik were widened and Nashik's first flyover was constructed near the Nasik Road railway station as part of the preparations for the Kumbha Mela. Twelve years later, around 629 km of roads were constructed, repaired, or widened in and around Nashik and seven new bridges were constructed. For the 2016 Ujjain Kumbha, as many as thirteen new flyovers and eleven new roads were constructed in and around Ujjain.

For the Prayaga Kumbha, the Public Works Department (PWD) of the Government of Uttar Pradesh is in charge of laying roads in and around Prayagraj and the Kumbha Nagari in addition to laying bridges. The main roads in the Kumbha Nagari are permanent or *pucca* in the sense their names and alignment are the same in every iteration of the Prayaga Kumbha. Even though their lines are erased when the Mela is not being held, the residents of Prayagraj remember their names and alignment. In 2013, around 160 km of *pucca* roads were constructed in the central, non-flooding area of the Kumbha Nagari using bitumen and chequered plates, called *charkhanedar plate* (चारखानेदार प्लेट) in Hindi. Chequered plates were used for the first time in 2013 to prevent the roads from getting slippery. Around 75,000 1m × 5m steel plates were sourced from Steel Authority of India Limited (SAIL). The plates were joined with bolts. The length of *pucca* roads laid was around 100 km in 2001 and 120 km in 2007 (year of the Ardha Kumbha). The steel plates were also used to create a large platform at the Sangama so that the *akhara* heads could bring their makeshift chariots (vehicles) right up to the Sangama. In addition to the *pucca* roads, smaller temporary roads were made of poured sand (a natural material) in the flooding areas. Sand provides good drainage and returns to the riverbed during the monsoon. These *pucca* and *kaccha* roads together make up the road network of the Kumbha Nagari at Prayaga.

An unmissable part of the ephemeral megacity at Prayaga are the temporary floating pontoon bridges (*pipa puls*) to facilitate crossing of the rivers by people and vehicles. The bridges are made of *pipas* (पीपा), hollow and cylindrical floating steel structures. In 2013, eighteen such bridges were laid across the Ganga and the Yamuna using more than 4,200 *pipas*. In the 2019 Ardha Kumbha, twenty-two pontoon bridges were put up while the 2025 Kumbha will have thirty pontoon bridges.

In the 2013 Kumbha, each *pipa* was 32 feet long, 8 feet wide, weighed 5.5 tonnes, and had two inspection cameras on top for monitoring the quality and performance of the waterproofing system. The *pipas* were manually pushed from the river banks to their final location by around 50 labourers. They were placed five metres apart and anchored on both sides using bamboo tripods which were embedded at the bottom of the river using sand bags. The *pipas* were connected with each other using two cables, a steel cable above water and a coir rope under water. The *pipas* were then covered with wooden decks, hay, mud, sand, and finally chequered steel plates to yield motorable bridges. Each bridge could handle a load of 10 metric tonnes (MT) but a limit of 5 MT was enforced. On the busiest days of the Mela, each bridge was monitored by a team of 35 people, including two junior engineers and an assistant engineer, for inspections and repairs. The longest of the eighteen pontoon bridges covered a span of 725 metres. Nine such bridges were laid in the 1989 Kumbha and thirteen in the 2001 Kumbha. The pontoon bridges are never seen empty during the Prayaga Kumbha, as M. Darrol Bryant observed in 1989 and as I noticed in 2013 and 2019. Pontoon bridges are used at other Kumbha Melas also. Seven pontoon bridges were built across the Shipra for the 2016 Ujjain Kumbha. Of these, five were laid by more than 150 jawans of the Indian Army working with 115 engineers. The Indian Army jawans took one day to build one bridge, and each bridge could bear a load of

50 MT. The bridges were put up at Lal Pul Ghat, Gandharva Ghat, Narasimha Ghat, Guru Nanak Ghat, and Sunahari Ghat. Two more bridges were laid at Jantar Mantar Ghat and Bhukhi Mata Ghat by the Madhya Pradesh Public Works Department (PWD) working with the Ujjain administration. Each bridge had a capacity of 20 MT and took around one week to be constructed. The *pipas* are often reused across melas. At the 2013 Prayaga Kumbha, around 2,700 new *pipas* were built and around 1,500 were reused from previous Kumbha Melas at Haridwar, Prayaga, Nashik, and Ujjain. Similarly, the two bridges laid by Madhya Pradesh PWD during the 2016 Ujjain Kumbha used *pipas* brought from Prayagraj.

To better manage the bathing crowds, sometimes old ghats are upgraded and new ghats are constructed before the Kumbha Mela. In 2003, the ghat at Rama Kunda, the traditional bathing spot of Vaishnava sadhus in Nashik, was concretized before the Mela. Several new ghats were constructed in Nashik for the 2015 Kumbha. Both local residents of Nashik and visiting *tirthayatris* found them to be beautifully done, cleanly maintained, less crowded, and well-managed. People were encouraged to bathe at the new ghats instead of Rama Kunda which was quite crowded. Similarly, several new bathing ghats were constructed along an eight-km stretch of the Shipra for the 2016 Ujjain Kumbha.

Medical Facilities

An event of the scale of the Kumbha Mela with crores of people bathing in river waters can easily become a tragedy if a disease or epidemic breaks out. There were several cholera outbreaks during Kumbha Melas in the previous century. For a long time, cholera inoculation was compulsory in Kumbha Melas, e.g. in the 1965 and 1977 melas at Prayaga. With improvement in health awareness and medical facilities at the Kumbha Mela, there has not been any major disease outbreak during the melas in recent times. The compulsory cholera inoculation is now a thing of the past. I was not inoculated for any of the four Melas (three Kumbha Melas and one Ardha Kumbha) I visited.

Provision of adequate medical facilities at the Kumbha Melas is a Herculean task. The task is most daunting at the Prayaga Kumbha, where the number of *tirthayatris* is the highest. During the 2013 Prayaga Kumbha, medical facilities were made available at multiple levels in the Kumbha Nagari for the entire duration of the Mela. The first level comprised 22 first aid centres. Each centre had one AYUSH (Ayurveda, Yoga and Naturopathy, Unani, Siddha, and Homoeopathy) specialist, one pharmacist, and an inpatient ward with two beds. At the next level were fourteen 24/7 allopathic hospitals, set up in different sectors of the Kumbha Nagari. Each hospital had five to six doctors, six to seven nurses, a pharmacy which provided free medicines, an Outpatient Department (OPD), and at least 20 beds for inpatient treatment. On average, the OPDs saw between 250 to 300 patients every day. Two hospitals were designated for treating infectious diseases. The central hospital in sector 2 had 70 doctors, a 100-bed inpatient unit, and a two-bed Intensive Care Unit (ICU) along with several departments (Orthopaedics, Medicine, Surgery, Eye Care, Skincare, and Obstetrics) and facilities (X-ray, Ultrasound, ECG, and medical laboratory). Seventy ambulances were stationed in the Kumbha Nagari with designated safe passages for emergencies. In all, there were 250 doctors including specialists and AYUSH practitioners inside the Kumbha Nagari. At the next level, one hundred beds were reserved for patients coming from the Mela at the Swaroop Rani Nehru Hospital in Prayagraj city. Around four lakh people were treated at the Mela for various types of ailments including asthma, diabetes, age-related problems, blood pressure, and accidents. In a study published in *PLOS Currents Diasters* in 2015, seven researchers from Tata Institute of Social Sciences (TISS) and Doctors For You (DFY) wrote that they found the health care conditions to be satisfactory at the 2013 Prayaga Kumbha.

Similar arrangements are made at the other Kumbha Melas. At the 2015 Nashik-Tryambakeshwar Kumbha, more than 1,250 doctors and paramedics were deployed. One permanent and thirty-two temporary hospitals were set up. Around 1.85 lakh people were examined and treated in the temporary hospitals over the duration of the Mela. ICUs with basic facilities including cardiopulmonary resuscitation (CPR) instruments were set up on all major bathing ghats. A man who had drowned was resuscitated in a ghat ICU and then transferred to a hospital for stabilization. Emergency routes were marked using which patients could be transferred to medical centres quickly.

A new initiative in medical services at the Kumbha Mela was the implementation of a telemedicine project at the 2016 Ujjain Kumbha. A telemedicine van manned with paramedical staff was stationed in Ujjain and patients coming to the van were treated by doctors in Lucknow and Bhopal (see chapter 8 for details).

Lost and Found

It is not uncommon for people, especially children and the old, to get separated from their family or groups and be lost in the crowd at a mass gathering event like the Kumbha Melas. Elaborate arrangements are made for helping unite lost people with their family or group. At the 2013 Prayaga Kumbha, there were 17 lost and found centres (*Bhule Bhatke Kendra*s) where people separated from their families could report themselves. The *kendra* would then make repeated announcements on loudspeakers and also put up the picture of the lost person on display screens and a website. On average, around 1,000 children were lost every day at the Mela and most of them were reunited with their families, except for one or two unfortunate children per day whose families could not be traced. Loudspeakers made repeated announcements about lost people and one camp was set up especially for looking after people who were lost. In some rare cases, people were lost for years. A 62-year-old farmer from Barmer in Rajasthan who had gone missing at the 2013 Kumbha was reunited with his family after five years in 2018. As will be shown in chapter 8, a successful experiment involving state-of-the-art technology and a volunteer force speaking multiple languages ensured that everybody who was lost at the 2015 Nashik Kumbha was reunited with their family or group.

Water, Sanitation, and Hygiene

Provision and maintenance of safe WASH (water, sanitation, and hygiene) conditions in the Kumbha Nagari is another major challenge for the administration. WASH conditions have greatly improved at the Kumbha Mela in recent times as India has made rapid strides towards eliminating open defecation with the Swachh Bharat Mission.

At the Prayaga Kumbha, the Uttar Pradesh Jal Nigam is responsible for providing clean drinking water. In 2013, the Jal Nigam supplied running water supply round the clock to *shiviras*, hospitals, police stations, and fire stations in the Kumbha Nagari. On average, 45 litres of water was made available per person per day. For ensuring this, around 550 km of water pipelines were laid and 42 pumps were set up. Contrast this with 1989, when around 180 km of water pipes were laid and 23 tube wells were set up. Around eight crore litres of drinking water was made available in 2013. Of this, five lakh litres (0.625%) was provided free of cost by Tata Chemicals, in partnership with the Uttar Pradesh Jal Nigam (see chapter 8). The quality of water supplied was regularly tested by both the Jal Nigam and Health Department by conducting orthotolidine tests for residual chlorine at more than 20 randomly chosen sites, twice a day.

The Uttar Pradesh Jal Nigam also has the responsibility of sewage disposal at the Prayaga Kumbha. For the 2013 Mela, around 40,000 portable toilets were put up. Diego Buñuel of the National Geographic found the toilet he used to be "super clean", although without toilet paper (most Indians prefer water to toilet paper). In addition, the Jal Nigam introduced zero-discharge mobile toilets: 630 of them were set up to dissuade people from open defecation. Compare this with the 1989 Kumbha when only 4,000 flush lavatories and 700 commodes were put up and open defecation was much more prevalent—human picking squads were deployed to remove all human excreta in the morning. In 2013, bleaching and fogging was done regularly by the Jal Nigam to control pests. Almost all *shivira*s had garbage pits for waste disposal. Around 6,000 sweepers were deployed and more than 200 tonnes of solid waste was removed from the Kumbha Nagari every day. The researchers from TISS and DFY wrote in *PLOS Currents Diasters* that they found the WASH conditions to be satisfactory at the 2013 Prayaga Kumbha and that the Mela was clean overall with few mosquitoes and flies. They recommended an improvement in drainage facilities, increasing the number of toilets, and providing separate toilets for men and women in the future.

In the 2019 Ardha Kumbha at Prayaga, more than 1.2 lakh eco-friendly toilets were set up. More than 20,000 sanitation workers were employed for cleaning the Kumbha Nagari. In addition, more than 1,500 *swachhagrahi*s (Clean India Mission volunteers) were deployed to monitor the cleanliness of the facilities and accommodations.

At the 2015 Nashik-Tryambakeshwar Kumbha, 39,000 toilets were put up and 32 km of water supply pipes and 27 km of drainage pipes were laid. The civic body deployed one sanitary employee at every 200 metres in addition to 170 extra garbage vans. One wheelbarrow was shared between two sanitary employees. Around 34,000 toilets, 10,000 urinals, and 15,000 bathrooms were built for the 2016 Ujjain Kumbha.

Food Supplies

At the 2001 Prayaga Kumbha, more than one lakh ration cards were issued. There were more than one hundred Public Distribution System (PDS) shops in the Kumbha Nagari through which 13,500 MT wheat, 7,800 MT rice, 5,000 MT sugar, and 11,000 kilolitre (KL) kerosene was made available at subsidized prices to the ration card holders. At the 2013 Prayaga Kumbha, more than two lakh ration cards were issued. There were 125 PDS shops in the Kumbha Nagari through which 16,200 MT wheat, 9,600 MT rice, 6,000 MT sugar, and 13,200 KL kerosene was made available to the card holders. Two hundred and five *lekhapalas* were assigned the tasks of making ration cards for the *tirthayatris*. The shops were spread across the sectors and were open from 8 am to 5 pm. In addition, there were around 150 milk distribution shops which sold 400 KL milk during the Mela, up from 106 shops selling 118 KL milk in 2001. In the upcoming 2025 Kumbha, 160 PDS shops will be set up in the Kumbha Nagari and an estimated two lakh ration cards will be issued. An unwritten rule is that no meat or alcohol is served in the Kumbha Nagari at Prayaga.

At the 2015 Nashik-Tryambakeshwar Kumbha, sadhus had requested the central government to provide foodgrain and LPG at subsidized rates to organize free *bhandaras*. The central government agreed. Seven PDS shops were set up, five at the *sadhugrama* in Nashik, and two at Tryambakeshwar. Instead of giving ration cards to *akharas*, establishment cards were given. Foodgrains were supplied through PDS shops to *akharas* which further distributed them to sadhus.

At the 2016 Ujjain Kumbha, there were 40 PDS shops which sold 6,000 MT wheat, 2,000 MT rice, and 1,000 MT sugar at subsidized prices.

Fuel Supplies

Over time, LPG and kerosene stoves have largely replaced wood and *gobar* (cow-dung) cakes used for cooking food at the Kumbha Mela, as observed by Mark Tully and G. C. Tripathi during the 1989 Prayaga Kumbha. For the 2001 Prayaga Kumbha, more than 7,000 LPG connections were issued and more than 33,000 cylinders were consumed. The number of connections sharply dropped to less than 1,000 at the 2013 Kumbha and only 4,000 cylinders were consumed till 13 February. This was largely due to the high price of LPG in market; organizations brought their own cylinders. The Oil Minister M. Veerappa Moily ordered subsidizing LPG on 13 February for the entire duration of the Mela. Diesel was also subsidized for boatmen. Around 25,000 LPG connections were issued during the 2015 Nashik-Tryambakeshwar Kumbha. At the 2016 Ujjain Kumbha, a Rs 100 subsidy was given on each cylinder to sadhus.

Security

The Kumbha Mela is prone to many security risks including stampedes and terrorist attacks. Elaborate security and police arrangements are required for maintaining law and order in the Kumbha Nagari and ensuring safety of lakhs of sadhus and crores of *tirthayatris*. These arrangements have grown with the size of the Mela in recent years. Given the largely religious and spiritual nature of the Mela, police forces are also expected to be respectful towards the sadhus and friendly towards the *tirthayatris*. During the Mela, many police personnel operate with a higher sense of duty, perhaps best captured in a candid conversation of an on-duty policeman at the 2010 Haridwar Kumbha in a Saregama Shakti documentary. After saying that all Haridwar policemen were working 12-hour shifts, he said that just like all *tirthayatris* were earning *punya* (merit) from the Mela, the policemen were earning *punya* by being on long duties.

At the 2010 Haridwar Kumbha, the state government had to request the central government and neighbouring states for additional forces to manage administration and security. Assisting the state police force were 800 personnel of the Central Reserve Police Force (CRPF), 200 personnel of the Rapid Action Force (RAF), and 400 personnel of the Central Industrial Security Force (CISF)—all three forces operate under the Union Ministry of Home Affairs (MHA). There were plans to deploy personnel from the Border Security Force (BSF) and the Indo Tibetan Border Police (ITBP) if a need arose. Seventeen new police outposts were set up on the Delhi–Haridwar national highway.

The Indian Army contributed in several ways to the 2013 Prayaga Kumbha. It opened up parts of Akbar's fort on the banks of the Yamuna near the Sangama for *tirthayatris*. The arrangement remained in place even after the Kumbha Mela was over. This gave *tirthayatris* access to the Patalpuri Mandir, Sarasvati Kupa, and the Akshaya Vata tree, all of which were inside defence land. The three places were also renovated at a cost of Rs 5 crore by the army. In addition, a control room was set up inside the fort where police and defence personnel kept a watch on the Kumbha Nagari. The army set up its own *shivira* near the Mela area with an aim of sharing its know-how in the fields of medicine, fire-fighting, and disaster response. Finally, the army set up small camps which could accommodate up to 300 people. Ex-servicemen visiting the Mela could stay in the camps for free.

In 2013, the Kumbha Nagari at Prayaga had 30 police stations, 12,500 police personnel, 36 companies of CISF, 25 companies of Provincial Armed Constabulary (PAC), and 4,500 Home Guards. In the previous Kumbha at 2001, the Kumbha Nagari had 28 police stations, 35 sub-stations, 10,000 police personnel, 35 companies of PAC, 3,000 Home Guards, and 400 chowkidars. At the 1989 Prayaga Kumbha, there were 21 police stations in the Kumbha Nagari with 7,000 police personnel. CCTV cameras were used for the first time in Prayaga at the Ardha Kumbha of 2007. Their number grew from 19 in 2007 to 85 in the 2013 Kumbha. In 2013, the police controlled over 3,000 public address (PA) systems and 56 CCTV cameras installed at important locations. CCTV footage was monitored round the clock by police personnel working in three shifts and was backed up for twelve days. A case study on the 2013 Prayaga Kumbha by the Bihar State Disaster Management Authority (BSDMA) stated that security at the Mela was "very tight". The Police had to step in during some very unusual situations. Naga Sarasvati, a sadhu of the Juna Akhara, had dug a ten-foot hole in which he planned to bury himself alive for nine days without oxygen, water, or food. The police had to physically prevent him from "committing suicide". The police have the additional task of ensuring that journalists do not disrupt the experience of the *tirthayatris*. When Diego Buñuel of the National Geographic started interviewing *tirthayatris* as they were bathing in the Sangama in 2013, a policeman rightly sent him away, asking him to shoot from a distance of 100 metres or take a boat.

    CCTVs have not only grown in number at the Kumbha Melas but have also become more sophisticated with time. At the 2010 Haridwar Kumbha, only 39 CCTV cameras were used. The 2013 Prayaga Kumbha had 85 CCTV cameras as stated earlier. At the 2015 Nashik-Tryambakeshwar Kumbha, 550 CCTV cameras were used. At the 2016 Ujjain Kumbha, 667 cameras were installed at 134 locations in the Mela area. Cisco Systems, the network partner for the city surveillance project in Madhya Pradesh, tied up with Honeywell to store and process the video data collected from these cameras. Cameras counting people and face detection cameras were put up at fourteen spots. The faces recognized were matched with stored images of history-sheeters and anti-social elements. Any resemblance would have triggered automatic alarms for the policemen monitoring the CCTVs. Automatic Number Plate Recognition (ANPR) cameras were put up at all roads leading to Ujjain. At the 2019 Prayaga Ardha Kumbha, more than 1,135 cameras were installed at 268 locations. There were two command and control centres with four viewing centres. An Integrated Command and Control Centre (ICCC) was set up to inspect the entire Mela. The ICCC housed 120 viewing operators, 30 call centre operators and 20 video wall cubes. This ICCC is being upgraded for the 2025 Kumbha Mela. In addition, two mini command centres are being set up at Arail and Jhunsi for better monitoring of the Mela.

Firefighting

Fire poses a great risk to life and property at the Kumbha Melas, especially since it can take a long time for fire brigades and firefighters to reach the fire due to the busy traffic and high density of people. Stray incidents of fire are known to occur at the Mela. One person was killed and twelve were injured when a fire broke out on 5 April at the 2010 Haridwar Kumbha. This was the first major tragedy of the 2010 Kumbha. Later in April, a forest fire in the Shivalik region reached the Hill Bypass road, Mansa Devi temple, and Bhimgoda in Kumbha Nagari and was approaching Haridwar city. While the Mela had ended, there were still many people in Kumbha Nagari for the bath on *Vaishakha Purnima* on 28 April. The fire was controlled before it could reach the city. In the 2021 Haridwar Kumbha, four incidents of fire were reported. In all cases, the fire was brought under control and there were no casualties.

At the 2013 Prayaga Kumbha, there were 30 fire stations with 47 fire-tenders, 426 firemen (including 100 leading firemen), 100 drivers, 21 fire officers, and eight chief fire officers in the Kumbha Nagari. For areas inaccessible by the fire-tenders, motorcycles and back-pack fire extinguishers were available for firemen. A total of 55 Motor Bike Fire Fighting Systems (MBFFS) were deployed. The fire department had one ambulance. The department provided fire extinguishers in all tents put up by the government. A major fire broke out in sector 11 on 15 January in which nineteen people sustained injuries. The fire was brought under control in half an hour and fortunately nobody was killed. In all, there were 612 fire incidents in the 2013 Mela which resulted in six deaths and fifteen burn injuries. The situation improved greatly in the 2019 Ardha Kumbha, with only 55 fire incidents and no deaths or burn injuries. In the 2019 Ardha Kumbha, 1,551 fire personnel and 166 fire vehicles were deployed. These numbers will be 2,071 and 351, respectively, in the 2025 Kumbha.

Twenty-two fire brigade teams were formed by the Nashik Municipal Corporation to deal with fires at the 2015 Nashik-Tryambakeshwar Kumbha. Four temporary fire stations were set up at the *sadhugrama* in Nashik in addition to the six existing fire stations. Eight fire brigade teams were deployed in Tryambakeshwar. Water mist units placed on motorcycles were made available for firefighting operations in the narrow and crowded lanes of Nashik and Trimbak. Diploma holders in Fire Engineering served as volunteers on the *shahi snana* days.

Thirty-seven fire stations were set up for the 2016 Ujjain Kumbha, which was held in peak summer season. Each sector had one or more fire stations and a team to supervise fire stations and fire order. The fire squad also inspected lighting arrangements at pandals, *shiviras*, and ashrams. Several fires broke out during the Mela. A massive fire broke out at the *shivira* of Chandrahamsa Maharaja in Pipli Naka on 18 May. Firefighters arrived late, an hour after the fire broke out, and extinguished the fire after several hours of effort. Nobody was killed but goods worth Rs 12 lakh were destroyed.

Electricity

The modern Kumbha Nagari at Prayaga is abuzz with activity even during the night. To a great extent, what makes this possible is the uninterrupted electric supply that powers the ephemeral city. At the 2013 Prayaga Kumbha, the Kumbha Nagari was divided into five electric zones with 52 electric sub-stations, each with two transformers of 400 kVA capacity. In addition, many mobile transformers were used. For connections between transformers and to the *shiviras*, 80 km of high-tension and 2,800 km of low-tension wires were used. The Kumbha Nagari had 24,000 street lights. As many as 140,000 free electricity connections were provided to different *shiviras*. The state and central governments bore most of the cost of the electricity, charging the users only a small amount of Rs 150 per connection. Safety was kept in mind while designing the electric system—no line carried more than 50 percent of its capacity. Every light cluster drew power from two sources and had a fail-safe mechanism where it would automatically switch within three seconds to the second source if one broke down. For emergency, forty-five generators of 63 kVA and 125 kVA capacity were arranged. Every alternate light cluster was run 24/7 using power drawn from these generators—the Mela would have had electricity and light even if there was a national grid failure. Three mock drills were conducted in December 2012 during which various sub-stations and power lines were alternately disabled to test for failure scenarios. At the 2019 Ardha Kumbha, around 2,80,000 electricity connections were provided to different *shiviras*. Fifty-four temporary sub-stations were deployed and around 40,700 LED lights and 175 high masts were placed.

A similar uninterrupted power supply was provided by the Madhya Pradesh Electricity Board (MPEB) during the 2016 Ujjain Kumbha. The government spent Rs 4 crore on installation of power cables and also bore the entire cost (around Rs 60 crore) of the power supply. Like in the 2013 Prayaga Kumbha, 45 generators were used for emergency. In case of a large power failure, there was plan to restore power within 15 minutes with a back-up supply from the Gandhi Sagar Dam.

Transport

To date, lakhs of people carry out the journey to the Kumbha Mela partially or completely on foot. Most people travelling on foot carry their necessary belongings in a bag of cloth on their head, "balanced in that remarkably graceful Indian way" as M. Darrol Bryant wrote of the *tirthayatris* in 1989. Bryant observed that most people in 1989 came on foot to Prayaga like Ram Sharma and five others who walked for 15 days from their village in Bihar. They would stay at the Mela for a week and then walk back home. In 2013, Indavara Gayathri, a *tirthayatri* from Bengaluru, similarly met a family which had walked from Bihar to Prayaga. With the increase in per capita income and road and rail connectivity, the proportion of people who come walking has gone down in the recent decades, though precise numbers are difficult to obtain.

Trains

Trains are perhaps the most common means of transport for *tirthayatris* visiting the Kumbha Mela today. For the 2013 Prayaga Kumbha, 750 special trains were run by North Central Railway (NCR). Thirty-seven Kumbha Mela special rakes were formed. Apart from running special trains, existing trains were modified with extra coaches—800 extra coaches were deployed by NCR and an additional 1,100 were deployed by Northern Railway (NR) and North Eastern Railway (NER). Goods traffic and parcel booking was restricted during the Mela at stations in and around Prayagraj. Eight long-distance trains were diverted to avoid passing through Prayagraj for some days. For the 2015 Nashik-Tryambakeshwar Kumbha, Central Railway (CR) ran ten special superfast trains between Nasik Road and Howrah and twenty special trains between Pune and Kamakhya. In 2004, 867 special trains were run for the Ujjain Kumbha. This number more than doubled to 2,190 special trains for the 2016 Kumbha. All trains halted at flag stations instead of the main railway station at Ujjain during the Mela. Two special trains were run between New Delhi and Haridwar during the 2016 Ardha Kumbha at Haridwar. In the 2019 Ardha Kumbha at Prayaga, more than 800 special trains were run by NCR for the visitors. For the 2025 Kumbha, 992 special trains will be run in addition to the 6,580 regular trains operating during the Mela.

Buses

Public transport operators arrange for special buses and sometimes even reduce fares on the bus routes during the Kumbha Mela. At the 2013 Prayaga Kumbha, around 900 regular and 3,600 special buses were run to and from Prayagraj for *tirthayatris*. The number was down from 8,000 buses in 1989, probably due to more people preferring to travel by trains or private transport in recent times. At the 2015 Nashik Kumbha, the Maharashtra State Road Transport Corporation (MSRTC) arranged for 3,000 buses for Nashik. Community radio system was installed in the buses through which the

Mela administration connected with *tirthayatris* travelling in them. Private buses were not allowed inside Nashik during the Kumbha Mela. At the 2016 Ujjain Kumbha, bus rides inside Ujjain were made completely free by the government on 28 April. The Atal Indore City Transport Service Limited (AICTSL), the public transport operator of Indore, arranged for 1,000 buses on the Indore-Ujjain route. The AICTSL deployed many school buses for transport as the Mela was held in April and May when most schools were closed for summer vacation.

Private transport

In recent years, the use of private transport has sharply increased among *tirthayatris* visiting the Kumbha Mela. Provision of adequate parking lots is a challenge owing to the high volume of private vehicular traffic. Ninety-nine parking lots were made available at the 2013 Prayaga Kumbha with a capacity of more than 3 lakh cars. This was 30 times more than the parking space available with thirty-five parking lots in 2001, reflecting the increase in use of private vehicles by *tirthayatris* over twelve years. At the 2015 Nashik-Tryambakeshwar Kumbha, 714 acres of parking space was provided for 20 parking lots. In 2016, 350 acres of parking space was provided in Ujjain for 12 new parking lots which were equipped with boom barriers, cameras, and bomb detection equipment. In the 2019 Ardha Kumbha at Prayaga, 120 parking lots for over six lakh vehicles were set up on an area of 1,291 hectares. For the 2025 Kumbha, the parking area will be much larger: 1,850 hectares.

Disaster Response

The organizers of the Kumbha Mela need to be prepared for any unforeseen disasters, natural or man-made. In 2006, India set up the National Disaster Response Force (NDRF) with the aim of specialized response to natural and man-made disasters. As of 2018, the NDRF consists of twelve battalions and more than a thousand personnel.

At the 2013 Prayaga Kumbha, the ninth battalion (9 Bn) of NDRF from Patna was deployed by the Uttar Pradesh government for the entire duration of the Mela. The battalion comprised navy and paramilitary personnel, who were trained for one month before becoming part of the team. The battalion was experienced in search and rescue operations and equipped with special diving equipment and motor boats. Other paramilitary forces were also present at the Mela.

In 2015, the Maharashtra government requested the Union government for involving the NDRF for disaster management at the Nashik-Tryambakeshwar Kumbha. The fifth battalion (5 Bn) of NDRF from Pune stationed two teams during the Mela at Nashik and Tryambakeshwar. The teams prepared several months in advance by visiting both places to collect first-hand information and meet with officials of all government agencies involved in managing the Mela. The NDRF team trained nearly 120 people including doctors, engineers, policemen, and government and civic body employees.

The eleventh battalion (11 Bn) of NDRF from Varanasi was deployed at the 2016 Ujjain Kumbha. NDRF personnel identified locations for potential stampede-like situations and informed the Mela administration of the same. During the

Mela, five teams with 235 NDRF personnel (including deep divers and paramedics) were stationed at five places. These personnel were trained for rescue operations in case of drowning, stampede, structural collapse, and fire accidents. They were equipped with boats, breathing jackets, stretchers, CSSR (Collapsed Structure Search and Rescue) equipment, and CBRN (Chemical, Biological, Radiological and Nuclear) equipment. On 5 May, a thunderstorm hit Ujjain grounding several pandals and killing seven people. Unfortunately, the NDRF team was late to arrive owing to a communication gap between the police control room and NDRF. Rescue operations were faster on 21 May when a fire broke out at the Ramsharan Gopal Ashram near the Mangalanatha Ghat. The NDRF team evacuated 15 persons and saved property worth Rs 15 lakh. Overall, NDRF personnel rescued 34 people during the Mela and retrieved one dead body. In the 2019 Ardha Kumbha at Prayaga, twelve NDRF teams of around 490 responders were deployed in various sectors and ghats to respond swiftly to emergencies. In addition, NDRF set up medical camps to provide primary health care facilities and also organized cleanliness drives. On 2 February, NDRF personnel rescued twelve *tirthayatris* from drowning after their boat capsized in the Ganga. In all, NDRF teams rescued nineteen *tirthayatris* during the Mela. At the 2025 Kumbha, thirty teams of NDRF and one team of State Disaster Response Force (SDRF), Uttar Pradesh, will be deployed for disaster relief.

Concluding Remarks

With awe-inspiring planning and management behind its organization, the Kumbha Mela is a wonder of modern-day management. At the Prayaga Kumbha, a temporary megacity is assembled and disassembled in just a few months. Kunal Pradhan of India Today called the Kumbha Nagari of the 2013 Prayaga Kumbha an "engineering miracle". Researchers from TISS and DFY found its planning and administration to be high-quality and said that the organizers were successful in supervising the event and making it "convenient, efficient, and safe". Planning and managing the Kumbha Mela requires deep collaboration between many government departments, police, doctors, engineers, firefighters, volunteers, and finally the sadhus and *tirthayatris*. They come and work together meticulously and miraculously, as if drawn by the *saṅgacchadhvam* spirit of the Mela, to make it a success.

4. Sadhus

The word sadhu (*sādhu*, साधु) is derived from the Sanskrit root √*sādh* which means "to completely accomplish [something]". A person who accomplishes *dharma* or *moksha* is a sadhu (*sādhnoti dharmaṃ mokṣaṃ veti sādhuḥ*). The word is used in Sanskrit for noble or good men and also for ascetics devoted to askesis. The feminine form of sadhu is *sadhvi* (साध्वी). Sadhus have been regarded very highly in the Indian tradition for a long time. The *Manu Smriti* says that the conduct of sadhus is one of the sources of *dharma* which is rooted in the Veda. In the *Gita*, Krishna says that he manifests himself for the protection of sadhus. In the *Bhagavata Purana*, Vishnu tells the sage Durvasas, "Sadhus are my heart and I am the heart of sadhus." In vernacular literature also, saints like Kabir and Tulasidasa have eulogized sadhus and their company.

In the context of Kumbha Melas and in this book, the word sadhu is exclusively used for ascetics who have renounced their families. Lakhs of sadhus live in India today; some estimates put their number at 50 lakh or even higher. To a great extent, the Kumbha Mela has been and continues to be a Mela of the sadhus. The Mela probably started as a meeting opportunity for sadhus, who live all year round in forests, caves, or mountains away from human settlements. They would come once every 12 years to a Kumbha Mela to meet with each other, to initiate new sadhus, to interact with common people, and to bathe in the Ganga, the Shipra, or the Godavari. Today, sadhus also settle organizational matters and disputes and conduct elections for their *akharas* at the Kumbha Mela.

Naga sadhus are an integral part of the Kumbha Melas. The Shaiva Nagas, present in thousands, are completely unclothed, even in the extreme cold weather during the Prayaga Kumbha. The Hindi word Naga (नागा) comes from Sanskrit *nagna* ("naked") or probably from Sanskrit *nāga* (नाग, "of the mountains"): Naga sadhus are both naked and live in the mountains. Jadunath Sarkar has written that it was the naked Naga sadhus who were called *gymnosophists* by Greeks historians including Arrian in *Indika* (second century BCE). While Shaiva Nagas stay naked all the time, Vaishnava and Udasina Nagas are *maryadita* ("bound by propriety")—they are clothed in the presence of people. Many Nagas, especially Shaiva Nagas, smoke charas (cannabis) in chillums (pipes made of clay). They believe it helps their concentration and sadhana.

Sadhus performing unbelievable ascetic feats in public gaze is a common sight at the Kumbha Melas even today. A spellbinding demonstration of advanced hatha yoga postures by the 86-year-old Amritananda Giri at the 1986 Haridwar Kumbha was captured on film in the documentary "Kings with Straw Mats". The effortlessness and speed with which the octogenarian sadhu moved from one difficult posture to the next amazes people even today. The same documentary showed a sadhu wearing iron bracelets weighing 25 kg in one arm. Some sadhus perform the *khadeshvari sadhana* in which they stand for many years. At the 1989 Prayaga Kumbha, Mark Tully wrote about Balayogi Baba who had stood on one leg for eight years. At the 2013 Prayaga Kumbha, Diego Buñuel interviewed Kailash Nath who had been standing on one leg for

10 years, with arms resting on a sling. Sadhus taking such a vow never experience deep sleep nor do they dream, as Kailash Nath told Buñuel. When asked what would he do when he would complete his vow of standing for twelve years, Kailash Nath simply said *"bhandara karenge ... bhajan karenge"* ("Will organize a public feast ... will sing bhajans"). Many sadhus believe in bhajan ("serving or worshipping the Lord") and *bhojan* ("feeding people") being two of their most important objectives. The *urdhvabahu* ("one with a raised arm") sadhu Bholanath Giri, who has never put down his left arm which he raised decades ago, is a regular visitor at Kumbha Melas. Some sadhus demonstrate *linga kriya*, in which they lift another sadhu, pull a vehicle full of sadhus, or lift a weight of many bricks using the penis. Often, a metal rod is rolled around the stretched foreskin for this purpose. Another common sight is a sadhu walking with slippers of pointed nails or lying on a bed of nails or thorns. There are sadhus who never set foot on the ground but perform *urdhvavasa* ("living above") all the time by staying on a swing or a raised platform (*machan*). The silent Tatamari Maharaja had been reportedly sitting in front of a *dhooni* for twenty years when he arrived at the 2015 Kumbha in Nashik. Also present in the same Kumbha at Nashik was Bhumi Baba or 'Underground Baba', who has been living in a small brick cave, partly in the ground and partly above, since 1997. At the 2016 Ujjain Kumbha, the six-foot-tall Janakidasa Tyagi demonstrated lifting a 15 kg gas cylinder with bricks placed on top of it using his 7.5-foot-long beard. Many *tirthayatris* gather around such sadhus to pay respect. Needless to say, all these feats are possible only after years of dedicated sadhana.

A lot has also changed about the sadhus at the Kumbha Melas in recent years. The deer skins and leopard skins, often seen as the *asana* (sitting mat) of sadhus in old photos, are no longer commonly seen. Mark Tully wrote about one Juna Akhara ascetic sitting on leopard skin in 1989. I have seen many sadhus at four Kumbha Melas but none with deer or leopard skin. In fact, I have seen only one sadhu in my life with deer skin—at Kamadagiri in Chitrakoot. Today, many sadhus at Kumbha Melas own smart phones and laptops. Namadeva Dasa Tyagi, a Vaishnava sadhu who is a regular at the Kumbha Melas, is popularly called 'Computer Baba' as he always carries a laptop with him. The Times of India reported that many Naga sadhus at the 2015 Nashik Kumbha were active on WhatsApp and Facebook using smart phones that were gifted to them by common people. While their life still largely revolves around meditation and sadhana, sadhus use social media to stay in touch with other sadhus and to check any updates posted by the gurus and acharyas of their *akharas*.

Popular Sadhus and Saints

For a long time, legendary saints of India have added to the glory of the Kumbha Mela with their presence. As per Paramahamsa Yogananda's autobiography, Yukteshwara Giri had met Mahavatara Babaji for the first time at the 1894 Prayaga Kumbha. Anandamayi Ma attended many Kumbha Melas in the last century, starting from the 1927 Haridwar Kumbha. In the 1936 Ardha Kumbha at Prayaga, Paramahamsa Yogananda met Krishnananda, the saint who had a vegetarian lioness as a pet. In the same year, the 43-year-old Yogananda briefly met with the 27-year-old Karapatra Swami (also known as Swami Karapatri), who was "noted for his exceptional intelligence". In the cold of 5–10°C, Karapatra Swami had just an ochre robe—no other clothes, no begging bowl, and no money. Later in his life, Karapatra Swami would be hailed as *Abhinava Shankaracharya* ("the modern Shankaracharya"). He would author many exceptional works including a brilliant Sanskrit commentary on the *Vajasaneyi Madhyandina Samhita* of the Shukla Yajur Veda and would even co-author a book which dealt with when the Kumbha Mela is to be held. Neem Karoli Baba is said to have attended the Prayaga Kumbha in 1966. Devaraha Baba attended many Kumbha Melas in the twentieth century. His last awe-inspiring presence was at the 1989 Prayaga Kumbha during which one of his public addresses was documented by Mark Tully. Tridandi Swami made his last appearance at the age of 93 at the 1998 Haridwar Kumbha. Mata Amritanandamayi, the hugging saint from Kerala, participated in her first Kumbha Mela at Prayaga in 2013. Barfani Dadaji organized a *samashti bhoja* ("attainment feast") for 20,000 sadhus at the end of the 2016 Ujjain Kumbha. Many other highly respected saints of India like have attended the Kumbha Mela regularly and continue to do so.

Akharas

The Hindi word *akhara* (अखाड़ा), also transliterated as *akhada*, means an arena for a sport. Most commonly used for a wrestling-field, the word is also used metaphorically for any competitive stage, e.g. *rajaniti ka akhara* ("the arena of politics"). The 13 organizations of sadhus that have traditionally participated in the Kumbha Mela are also called *akharas*. The word does not mean a "circle", as a *Newsweek* article on the 2013 Kumbha incorrectly stated. Several scholars opine that *akhara* comes from Sanskrit *akhanda* ("complete"), however this is untenable as there is no relation between the meanings. Some others suggest that the origin is in Sanskrit *āmnāya* (आम्नाय), however the words sound too different to have any relation. The most likely derivation of the word *akhara* is from Prakrit *akkhāḍaya* (अक्खाडय), a variant form of *akkhāḍaga* (अक्खाडग), which in turn comes from Sanskrit *akṣavāṭaka* (अ-क्षवाटक). The word *akṣa* refers to a die used in gambling, while *vāṭaka* means an enclosure. So *akṣavāṭaka* in Sanskrit means "an enclosure for gambling", which is also the meaning of the word *akkhāḍaya* in Prakrit. Over time the word *akkhāḍaya* and its later form *akhara* came to mean an enclosure for wrestling or a sporting arena.

While many sadhus, especially Shaiva sadhus, believe that it was Adi Shankaracharya who first organized sadhus into *akharas*, some scholars hold the view that sadhus organized themselves into *akharas* during the Islamic rule of India for their protection. In addition to learning scriptures (*shaastra-vidya* or शास्त्रविद्या), they started practising martial arts (*shastra-vidya* or शस्त्रविद्या) also and so their organizations came to be known as *akharas*, or arenas for martial arts.

For a long time, 13 *akharas* (seven Shaiva, three Vaishnava, two Udasina, and one Sikh) have traditionally participated in the Kumbha Melas. For quite some time, they were represented in the *Akhil Bharatiya Akhara Parishad* (ABAP). In 2021, the ABAP split into two factions. There were reports of a truce between the two factions in September 2024, but in November

2024, Vaishnava sadhus formed a new entity called the *Akhil Bhartiya Vaishnava Akhara Parishad*.

A brief description of the thirteen *akharas* follows next.

Shaiva *akharas*

Shaiva *akharas* comprise Shaiva sadhus, worshippers of Shiva who wear the horizontal mark called *tripundra* (त्रिपुण्ड्र) on their forehead. They include *dashanami samnyasis* who are followers of Adi Shankaracharya. The seven Shaiva *akharas* are the first to take bath on special bathing days (*shahi snana* days) at the Prayaga Kumbha. They march in the following order—the Mahanirvani along with the Atala *akhara*, the Niranjani along with the Ananda *akhara*, and finally the Juna along with the Avahana and Agni *akharas*.

1. Mahanirvani Akhara

Mahānirvāṇī (महानिर्वाणी) is a Sanskrit word which means "endowed with great liberation". The *Shri Panchayati Akhara Mahanirvani* (Mahanirvani Akhara) is believed to have been founded in the eighth century. It is based at Daraganj in Prayagraj and has centres at many places including Kankhal, Khandwa, and Baroda. The *akhara* has many Naga sadhus. It is the mahants of this *akhara* who perform the famed *bhasma-arati* at the Mahakala Jyotirlinga temple in Ujjain. The *akhara* worships sage Kapila as its *kulaguru* and celebrates *Kapila Jayanti* (the appearance day of Kapila) with great fervour. According to the *Bhagavata Purana*, Kapila is the fifth avatara of Vishnu and the propounder of the *Sankhya* philosophy.

2. Atala Akhara

Aṭala (अटल) is a Sanskrit word which means "unwavering, resolute, or firm". The *Shri Shambhu Panchayati Atala Akhara* (Atala Akhara) is based in Varanasi and has many centres across India including in Prayagraj, Baroda, Haridwar, Nashik, and Ujjain. This is one of the oldest *akharas*, believed to have been founded in the seventh century CE. It is also one of the smallest, it had around five hundred sadhus as of 2016. The *ishta* deity of this *akhara* is Ganesha. For a long time, the *akhara* accepted only males from the three *varnas* (Brahmanas, Kshatriyas, and Vaishyas) in its fold.

3. Niranjani Akhara

The Sanskrit word *niranjanī* (निरञ्जनी) means "with the unblemished [Brahman or OM]." The *Panchayati Akhara Shri Niranjani* (Niranjani Akhara) is believed to have been founded in Gujarat during the tenth century. Like the Mahanirvani Akhara, it is based at Daraganj, Prayagraj. Its centres are in Haridwar, Varanasi, Trimbak, Omkareshwar, Ujjain, and Udaipur. Even though the worship of Karttikeya (Murugan) among the masses is not very common outside southern India, Karttikeya is the *ishta* deity of the Niranjani Akhara. At the 2013 Prayaga Kumbha, the welcome arch of the *akhara*'s *shivira* had Karttikeya and Shiva depicted prominently on either side of its name. As of 2016, the *akhara* had fifty Mahamandaleshvaras, most of whom were well-educated sadhus.

4. Ananda Akhara

Ānanda (आनन्द) is a common Sanskrit word meaning "bliss". The *Shri Taponidhi Ananda Akhara Panchayati* (Ananda Akhara) is believed to have been founded in the ninth century CE in Berar. The *akhara* does not have any Mahamandaleshvaras but only acharyas. The *ishta* deity of the *akhara* is Surya. The *akhara* is based in Trimbak and has several centres in India. Many sadhus of this *akhara* live in Varanasi. Every six years, in the Ardha Kumbha or the Purna Kumbha, the *panchas* (leaders) of this *akhara* are elected. Like the Atala Akhara, the Ananda Akhara also accepted only males from the three *varnas* in its fold until recently. The *akhara* places high emphasis on scriptural knowledge.

5. Juna Akhara

Juna (जूना), from Sanskrit *jīrṇa* (जीर्ण) or *jūrṇa* (जूर्ण), is a Hindi word meaning "old". The *Shri Pancha Dashanama Juna Akhara* (Juna Akhara) is believed to be the oldest of all *akharas*, although some other sources say it was founded in the eleventh century CE. It was known in the past as *Bhairava Akhara* when its *ishta* deity was Bhairava, a form of Shiva. Today, its *ishta* deity is Dattatreya, a *samaveta avatara* (combined incarnation) of Brahma, Vishnu, and Shiva. The *akhara* is based in Varanasi and has many branches and centres across India. The *Juna Akhara* is the largest *akhara* with an estimated five lakh sadhus today. In 2016, the *akhara* had nearly 300 Mahamandaleshvaras, including several foreigners and women. At the Kumbha Mela, the arch of its camp carries depictions of Dattatreya and a *kumbha*. The Sanskrit phrase *śrīdattātreyo vijayatetarām* ("Utmost glory to the auspicious Dattatreya") is written on its banners. The highly respected Swami Avadheshananda Giri is the Acharya Mahamandaleshvara of the Juna Akhara.

6. Avahana Akhara

The word *āvāhana* (आवाहन) means "invocation [of a deity]" in Sanskrit. The *Shri Pancha Dashanama Avahana Akhara* (Avahana Akhara) is based at the famous Dashashvamedha Ghat at Varanasi and has centres in Haridwar, Nashik, Ujjain, and Junagadh. Based on a record in a *pothi*, it is believed to have been founded in the sixth century or, as per Jadunath Sarkar, in the sixteenth century if the figure for one thousand in the year has been omitted. Until recently, the *Avahana Akhara* did not admit women in its fold. The sadhus of the *akhara* have two *ishta* deities—Ganesha and Dattatreya. Both are believed to have manifested themselves as a result of *āvāhana* or invocation.

7. Agni/Panchagni Akhara

Agni (अग्नि), the first word of the Rig Veda's *samhita*, is the name of the Vedic fire deity. The Sanskrit word *panchagni* (पञ्चाग्नि) means "five fires" and is possibly a reference to the *panchagni vidya* of the *Chandogya* and *Brihadaranyaka* Upanishads. The *Shri Pancha Dashanama Panchagni Akhara* (Agni or Panchagni Akhara) is based at Bhavnath village in Junagadh and has centres at several other places in India. Only Brahmins who are *brahmacharins* are initiated in the *akhara*. The *akhara* is relatively small and has around four to five thousand sadhus and saints. They are associated with one of the four Shankara *peethas*, whose Shankaracharyas are also members of this *akhara*. The *brahmacharins* associated with Jyotirmatha, Shringeri, Govardhana, and Dwarika *peethas* have *Ananda*, *Chaitanya*, *Prakasha*, and *Svarupa* respectively as a part of their name. The *ishta* deity of this *akhara* is

Gayatri. Sadhus of the *akhara* do not maintain a *dhooni*. The current Mahamandaleshvara of the *akhara* is Brahmarshi Ramakrishnananda, based at Amarkantak in Madhya Pradesh.

Vaishnava *akharas*

The three Vaishnava *akharas* are also called *anis*. Ani (अणि or अनी) is an Awadhi word which means "an army" and comes from Sanskrit *anīka* (अनीक). Traditional accounts say that Vaishnava sadhus were organized into seven *akharas* by Balananda in the eighteenth century. The *akharas* grew in number over time and were re-organized into three *ani akharas*. All the three *ani akharas* have an image of Hanuman on their flags. Vaishnava sadhus wear the *urdhvapundra* ("vertical mark") on their forehead and belong to one of the four *sampradayas* (Nimbarka, Madhva, Vishnuswami, and Shri). At the Prayaga Kumbha, Vaishnava *akharas* march after the Shaiva *akharas* in the following order.

8. Nirvani Akhara

The word *nirvāṇī* (निर्वाणी) means "liberated" in Sanskrit. The *Shri Panch Nirvani Ani Akhara* (Nirvani Akhara) is based at Hanumangarhi in Ayodhya. It is believed to have been founded in the eighteenth century by Abhayaramadasa. The *akhara* is sub-divided into four *pattis* (पट्टी, "strips" or "bands") named Sagariya, Basantiya, Ujjainiya, and Haridwari. The *akhara* holds *nagapana* (नागापना, "nakedness") programmes at the Kumbha Melas where new Naga sadhus are initiated. The Sagariya and Ujjainiya *pattis* hold their *nagapana* programme during the Haridwar Kumbha while the Basantiya and Haridwari *pattis* do the same during the Ujjain Kumbha. The *akhara* has a red triangular flag. It is known for its continued emphasis on physical fitness and wrestling. Out of the 1,500 sadhus staying in its camp at the 2016 Ujjain Kumbha, 300 were former or current wrestlers. The wrestler sadhus wake up at 3 am every day, run around ten kilometres, and practise wrestling before sunrise, after which their sadhana begins. Some sadhus have even won wrestling titles like *Bihar Kesari*, *Uttar Pradesh Kesari*, and *Bharat Kesari* in the past.

9. Digambara Akhara

The word *digambara* (दिगम्बर) means "having directions as clothes", i.e. naked, in Sanskrit. The *Shri Panch Ramanandiya Digambara Ani Akhara* (Digambara Akhara) was founded by Balaramadasa in the eighteenth century, some others claim its formation dates to the fourteenth century by Balanandacharya and Ramanandacharya. The *ishta* deities of this *akhara* are Sita and Rama, who are worshipped with Hanuman. There are two sub-*akhara*s, the *Rama Digambara* and *Shyama Digambara*, with seats at Ayodhya, Chitrakoot, Nashik, Puri, Ujjain, and Vrindavan. This is the largest Vaishnava *akhara* with around two lakh sadhus in 450 *khalsas* across India. It has a five-coloured rectangular flag with white, red, black, green, and yellow stripes.

10. Nirmohi Akhara

The word *nirmohi* (निर्मोही) means "without ignorance" in Sanskrit. The *Shri Panch Ramanandiya Nirmohi Ani Akhara* (Nirmohi Akhara) has nearly 1.25 lakh sadhus organized in around 150 *khalsas* across India. It is based in Chitrakoot and has centres in Ayodhya, Nashik, Puri, Ujjain, and Vrindavan. It has a white triangular flag with a golden border. The Nirmohi Akhara was one of the three litigants in the Rama Janmabhumi-Babri Masjid title suit.

Udasina *akharas*

The Sanskrit word *udāsīna* (उदासीन) means "indifferent" or "neutral". True to their name, Udasina sadhus are neutral, i.e. neither completely Shaiva nor completely Vaishnava and neither completely Hindu nor completely Sikhs. They explain the word *udāsīna* as "seated above" (*ud* = "above" and *āsīna* = "seated"), i.e. "seated in Brahman". They march after the Shaiva and Vaishnava *akharas* during the bathing procession at the Prayaga Kumbha.

11. Bada Udasina Akhara

Bada (बड़ा) means "large" in Hindi. The *Shri Panchayati Akhara Bada Udasina Nirvana* (Bada Udasina Akhara) is based in Prayagraj and has 17 branches across India. The *akhara's* banners have *svastika*, the sacred Hindu symbol, and OM, depicted in the Hindu style (ॐ). Sadhus of the *akhara* revere Udasinacharya and Chandracharya (the Sanskritized name of Sri Chanda, the elder son of Guru Nanak). The Udasina sadhus believe that Chandracharya was a master in a long line of Udasina teachers. The *akhara* is believed to have been founded in the late eighteenth century by Priyatamadasa Maharaja. Its motto is "cheto nagari taaro gaanv, alakh purush ka sumiro naanv" (चेतो नगरी तारो गाँव, अलख पुरुष का सुमिरो नाँव), which means, "Awaken the city and redeem the village, remember the name of the invisible Purusha." Reflecting its Shaiva-Vaishnava syncretism, the *akhara* organized *kathas* on both *Shiva Purana* (a Shaiva Purana) and *Bhagavata Purana* (a Vaishnava Purana) in addition to staging *Krishna Lila* programmes at the 2016 Ujjain Kumbha.

12. Naya Udasina Akhara

The Hindi word *naya* (नया) means "new". The *Shri Panchayati Akhara Naya Udasina* (Naya Udasina Akhara) branched out from Udasina sadhus in the early twentieth century. It is based in Prayagraj and has 27 centres in places like Amritsar, Haridwar, Nashik, Patiala, Tryambakeshwar, Ujjain, and Varanasi. The *akhara* has the tradition of offering *madira* (liquor) to fire. A unique feature of this *akhara* is its tradition of initiating children as Naga sadhus. Till the end of the last century, the *akhara* used to admit 30–40 children, many of them orphans who would voluntarily come to the *akhara*, at every Kumbha Mela. In 2013 (Prayaga) and 2015 (Nashik), the *akhara* initiated only adults as no children came forward to become sadhus. The *akhara* believed this to be an impact of changing times where many social organizations are taking care of destitute children.

Sikh *akhara*

Like I was in 2013, many first-time visitors to the Kumbha Mela are surprised to notice the *shivira* of the Nirmala Sikhs with the *ik omkar* (ੴ) signs. The Nirmala Akhara is the last *akhara* to march in the bathing procession of sadhus at the Prayaga Kumbha.

13. Nirmala Akhara

The Sanskrit word *nirmala* (निर्मल) means "sinless" or "immaculate". The *Shri Panchayati Akhara Nirmala,* (Nirmala Akhara) is based in Kankhal (Haridwar) and has around 15,000 sadhus with centres at many places. The sadhus of the *akhara* consider Guru Nanak to be the founder of their *sampradaya*. They trace the origin of their Sanskrit tradition to Guru Gobind Singh sending five saints from Paonta Sahib in current-day Himachal Pradesh to Varanasi for studying Sanskrit in 1686. The sadhus of the *akhara* shun all intoxicants. They revere both Hindu texts (Vedas, *Vedangas, Bhagavad Gita,* Upanishads) and the Sikh scripture (*Guru Grantha Sahib*). Some sadhus also study Sanskrit and recite Sanskrit verses in praise of Guru Nanak. Nirmala Akhara sadhus perform *arati* of the *Guru Grantha Sahib* with lamps the way Hindus perform *arati* of *murti*s. The followers of Nirmala Akhara are Nirmala Sikhs, who believe in a living guru and also bathe in sacred rivers unlike mainstream Sikhs. Nirmala Sikhs consider themselves to be Sikhs but not Singhs.

Marching order

The order of bathing for the *akhara*s is sometimes different from the established order at Prayaga. In the second *shahi snana* on 13 September at the 2015 Nashik-Tryambakeshwar Kumbha, the Nirmohi Akhara was the first to bathe at Rama Kunda, followed by Digambar and Nirvani Akharas. At the Kushavarta Kunda, the Niranjani Akhara was the first followed by Ananda, Juna, Agni, Avahana, Mahanirvani, Atala, Bada Udasina, Naya Udasina, and finally Nirmala Akhara.

Peshwai and flag-hoisting

Before the beginning of the Kumbha Mela, various *akhara*s march in the city as part of a ceremonial procession known as *peshwai* (पेशवाई), sometimes also called *praveshai* (प्रवेशाई). The *peshwai* is an occasion for residents of the city and *tirthayatris* to welcome the sadhus to the Kumbha Mela. Sadhus, who usually eat food only once a day, traditionally eat *khichdi* before the *peshwai* procession. The *peshwai* is no less than a royal procession—sadhus march with horses, elephants, and bands playing music. The Mahamandaleshvaras or Shri Mahantas of the *akhara*s are seated on vehicles converted into chariots during the *peshwai* in which Naga sadhus often display their acrobatic skills and martial skills with sticks, swords, and spears. The residents of the city and *tirthayatris* shower flowers on the sadhus and gift them garlands. At the 2010 Haridwar Kumbha, flowers were showered from a helicopter on the sadhus. The *peshwai* of the Juna Akhara, the largest *akhara*, is a major attraction. In the 2016 Ujjain Kumbha, the event was attended by the Chief Minister of Madhya Pradesh.

Shortly after the *peshwai*, a *dharma-dhvaja* ("flag of *dharma*") is hoisted by the *akhara*s. This raising of the flag marks the ceremonial beginning of the Kumbha Mela. The flag is lowered when the Mela ends. For the 2013 Prayaga Kumbha, the Vaishnava *akhara*s raised a 70-foot high *dharma-dhvaja* on 12 December 2012 (more than a month before the Mela started), after a long *bhumi-pujana* ceremony. At the 2015 Nashik-Tryambakeshwar Kumbha, flowers were showered from helicopters during the Vaishnava *akhara*s' flag-hoisting ceremony which was attended by the Maharashtra Chief Minister and the BJP President along with other dignitaries.

The flag raised at Nashik was made of five metals (*panchadhatu*) and had engravings of Guru (Jupiter), Surya (the Sun), Chandra (the Moon), Godavari, a crocodile (believed to be the mount of goddess Godavari), all directions, twelve zodiacs, and the *svastika*. The flag was hoisted at a height of 31 feet from the ground.

Battles between *akharas*

While sadhus were organized into *akharas* for the protection of Hindu monastic traditions and Naga sadhus also occasionally engaged with battles with Islamic militants, some Kumbha Melas in the past have seen unfortunate internecine battles between *akharas*. As per Captain Raper, around 18,000 sadhus (mostly Vaishnavas) died in a battle between Shaiva and Vaishnava sadhus for bathing first at the 1760 Haridwar Kumbha. The number was most probably exaggerated by Raper who wrote in 1808, almost half a century after 1760. Writing in 1909, R. Nevill put the number of casualties in the 1760 battle as only 1,800. At the 1796 Haridwar Kumbha, around 500 Shaiva sadhus were killed in a battle with Nirmala Sikhs. There have been some other such struggles between *akharas*, but these are exceptions in the centuries-old tradition of the Kumbha Mela. Today, the relations between Shaiva, Vaishnava, Udasina, and Sikh *akharas* are largely peaceful. In 2010, the thirteen *akharas* created history at the Haridwar Kumbha when all of them took part in the *Chaitra Purnima* bath which was hitherto considered a sacred bath by the Vaishnava *akharas* alone. Not only was this an example of the Shaiva *akharas* showing respect towards the Vaishnava *akharas*, it was also a means to demonstrate Hindu unity.

Nagas

Naga sadhus are initiated by all *akharas* at the Kumbha Melas. Shaiva Nagas are initiated by the hundreds at the Haridwar Kumbha in the Juna Akhara 2–3 days before each royal bath (*shahi snana*). The new initiates shave off all their hair and are then consecrated by a *pujari* (priest) who sprinkles water on them in the presence of an acharya. After this the initiates bathe in the Ganga. Then loincloths, *vibhuti* (ash), and *janeus* (sacred threads) are distributed among them. A *danda* (staff) is given to each new initiate to make them a *dandi samnyasi* ("renunciate with a staff"). After this, the initiates are made to give up their *danda* and perform a *havana* known as *Vijaya-havana* below the flag of the *akhara*. Then the Acharya Mahamandaleshvara makes them recite some Sanskrit mantras after which they give up the *janeu* also. The initiates then spend one night in silence (*mauna*), chanting OM in their minds. The next morning, they are given a mantra by the Acharya Mahamandaleshvara after which they become Naga sadhus. Hundreds of Shaiva Nagas are initiated at the Prayaga Kumbha too. Parts of the ceremony in 2013 were shown by Diego Buñuel of the National Geographic.

A major attraction at the Kumbha Mela, especially the Prayaga Kumbha, is the charge of the Shaiva Naga sadhus to bathe in the Sangama on the occasion of a royal bath (*shahi snana*). A special corridor is reserved for the Nagas to run. Crowds that line up for hours to witness the event are cleared using barricades by the police personnel, present in large numbers to keep the crowd in order. The sadhus run completely naked, covered only in ash (*bhasma*) smeared all over their body. All this happens in the presence of shouts of

Hara Hara Mahadeva and *Hara Hara Gange*, beats of dhols, and clicks of cameras. Some sadhus are tonsured, some are bald, while some have long matter hair till their feet. Some go to the river mounted on horses and some others mount the shoulders of other Naga sadhus. Some are young initiates and some are old men. Some break any cameras taking their photos while some happily pose for cameras. Some do not say a word and some speak even in English to the foreign onlookers. Some walk solemnly while some run like excited children. The people in the crowd keep throwing thousands of marigold flowers and garlands at the sadhus who put them around their head or neck. The joy on the faces of the Nagas as they plunge into the waters is beyond words. Many start playing in the river as a five-year-old child plays in the lap of his mother. Indeed, the Ganga is the mother to all Naga sadhus as it is a mother to the insects, the birds, the animals, and the devout living on her banks. This is the moment these children unite with their mother Ganga after waiting for years. Having forsaken all familial ties, desires, and worldly attachments, the Nagas come to meet their mother and experience a bliss that perhaps nothing else in the world could give them.

Vaishnava *akharas* also have Naga sadhus but they are *maryadita* ("bounded by propriety") and hence wear white or yellow robes (except for some *acharyas* who wear ochre robes). Due to this reason, they are also called *vastradhari* Nagas. The Vaishnava *akharas* initiate Naga sadhus from all *varnas* and *jatis* (castes), following the egalitarian principles laid down by Ramanandacharya who said *jaata paanta puchhe nahin koya, hari ko bhaje so hari ka hoya* ("Let none ask somebody's caste or rank, one who worships Hari belongs to Hari"). All Vaishnava sadhus are said to belong to the *achyuta gotra*, the *gotra* of Vishnu. Many Vaishnava Naga sadhus perform the difficult austerity called *dhooni sadhana* for 18 years (six phases of three years each). During this sadhana, they sit with a burning *dhooni* (धूनी) for several hours every day during spring and summer, chanting their mantra or meditating. The smoke and heat from the *dhooni* make the *tapas* ("penance" and also "heat") true to its name. The first phase is *pancha dhooni*, in which *kandas* (cow-dung cakes) are lit at five places around the sadhu. The second and third phases are *sapta dhooni* and *dvadasha dhooni* in which *kandas* are lit at seven and twelve places, respectively, around the sadhu. After this comes the fourth phase called *chaurasi dhooni* in which *kandas* are lit at 84 places in a large circle. The fifth phase is *kota dhooni* in which many *kandas* are placed and lit very close to each other in a circle around the sadhu. The Hindi word *kota* (कोट) in *kota dhooni* probably comes from Sanskrit *koṭi* (कोटि) which means "a crore" and also "uncountable". Or, perhaps it is the Hindi word *kota* meaning "a bulwark". The sixth and most difficult phase is *kota khappara* or *kota khopara* in which the sadhu sits with *kandas* burning in an earthen vessel on his head as well as a circle of burning *kandas* around him as in *kota dhooni*. Many Vaishnava sadhus come to perform different phases of *dhooni sadhana* at the Kumbha Melas—around 8,000 performed *dhooni sadhana* at the 2016 Ujjain Kumbha in the sweltering heat of 40°C.

Sampradayas

The Sanskrit word *sampradaya* (सम्प्रदाय), from the root √da ("to give"), refers to both the learning imparted in a lineage (*parampara*) of gurus and the group of people endowed with such learning. It is this latter sense in which the word is commonly used now. The Indian learning tradition places a lot of emphasis on obtaining knowledge through a *sampradaya*. In his commentary on the *Bhagavad Gita*, Adi Shankara says, "one who does not know *sampradaya* is to be ignored just like a fool, even if he knows all scriptures." The derivative word *sampradayika* (साम्प्रदायिक) simply means "based on tradition" in Sanskrit. Unfortunately, *sampradayika* is used in a negative sense in modern Hindi where it means "communal" and similarly *sampradayikata* (साम्प्रदायिकता) has the negative sense of "communalism" in modern Hindi.

For centuries, the Kumbha Mela is known for the presence of four Vaishnava *sampradayas*. They are sometimes referred to simply as four *sampradayas*. The other major *sampradaya* present at the Kumbha Mela is the Dashanami *sampradaya* of the Shaiva ascetics. The *Bitaka*, a work composed by Laladasa in 1694, mentions the participation of saint Prananatha of the *Pranami Sampradaya* in the 1678 Haridwar Kumbha Mela. The work says, "In the Mela of Haridwar there were four *sampradayas*; [scholars of] the six philosophical schools also met where there were *dashanami samnyasis*."

Historically, the *akhara* identified the military group or sub-group to which a sadhu belonged while the *sampradaya* identified his *parampara*, giving him two identities. For example, a sadhu would describe himself as a Nirvani of the Nimbarka *sampradaya*, as W. G. Orr writes.

Four *sampradayas*

The four Vaishnava *sampradayas* that have traditionally participated in the Kumbha Mela include the *Shri Sampradaya*, the *Rudra Sampradaya*, the *Sanakadi Sampradaya*, and the *Brahma Sampradaya*. In the *Bhaktamala* of Nabhadasa, the four *sampradayas* are called the four *vyuhas* (manifestations) of Hari (Vishnu) in the *Kali Yuga*.

(1) *Shri Sampradaya* includes the followers of Ramanuja (Ramanujis) and the followers of Ramananda (Ramanandis). They both follow the philosophy of *Vishishtadvaita* ("qualified monism") but their *ishta* deities and *mantras* are different. The Ramanujis worship Lakshmi and Vishnu while the Ramanandis, forming the largest Vaishnava monastic order in India, worship Sita and Rama. Although the followers of Ramanuja are most numerous in southern Indian states, it is the Ramanujis from northern India who are more conspicuous at the Kumbha Melas. Ramanuji sadhus like Swami Vasudevacharya and Lakshmiprapanna Jeeyar Swami and Ramanandi saints like Swami Hamsadevacharya, Swami Narendracharya, and Swami Ramabhadracharya have regularly participated in recent Kumbha Melas.

(2) *Rudra Sampradaya* historically included the followers of Vishnusvami who were later superseded and largely absorbed by the *pushtimargis*, followers of Vallabhacharya (1479–1531). The *pushtimargis* follow the philosophy of *Shuddhadvaita* ("pure monism") and are mostly found in western and central India today. They heartily participate in the Kumbha Melas. At the 2016 Ujjain Kumbha, around two lakh *pushtimargis* camped at the Vallabhacharya Nagar under Goswami Kalyana Raya Maharaja of the second *Shuddhadvaita peetha*. A *vigraha* of

Govardhananatha (a form of Krishna) was brought from Dahod in Gujarat and was offered various *manorathas* (*prasada* offerings, literally "wishes") on different days during the Mela.

(3) *Sanakadi Sampradaya* has the followers of Nimbarka who are mostly restricted to some places in Rajasthan and around Vrindavan in Uttar Pradesh. They follow the philosophy of *Dvaitadvaita* ("dualism and monism"). Currently, there is only one Nimbarkacharya Peetha left in India, that at Kishangarh in Ajmer (Rajasthan), with around ten lakh followers worldwide. At the modern Kumbha Melas, there is a small presence of the Nimbarka sadhus including *kathiya* ("carrying a wooden block") sadhus from the Bangiya Nimbarka Ashram (affiliated to the Nirvani Akhara) in West Bengal and sadhus of the *Sakhi Sampradaya*, an offshoot of the Nimbarka *sampradaya*.

(4) *Brahma Sampradaya* is the term used to refer to followers of Madhvacharya who are mostly found in southern India. They follow the philosophy of *Dvaita* ("dualism"). Not many Madhva sadhus and saints are present at Kumbha Melas in modern times, though textual accounts and oral traditions attest to their participation in history. Swami Vishvesha Tirtha of the Pejavar Mutt in Udupi used to visit the Kumbha Mela at times but only for a few days, especially when there a conference of saints would be held.

Other Vaishnava sadhus are also present at the Kumbha Mela. A notable example in recent past was Purushottama Goswami (1919–2017), the head priest of the Shri Radha Raman Mandir at Vrindavan and an acharya of Chaitanya *sampradaya*. He was a regular at the Prayaga Kumbha and was well-known for his insightful discourses on the spiritual significance of the Kumbha Mela.

Dashanami sampradaya

The *Dashanami* ("having [one of] ten names") *sampradaya* is the collective name given to the ten orders of Shaiva *samnyasis* which are believed to have been established by Adi Shankara. The *Dashanamis* often have a first name ending in *ananda*. Their last name is one of the below ten names. The descriptions of the names below are as per the *Mathamnaya Setu*, a work attributed to Adi Shankara (for the original verses, refer the appendix):

(1) *Tirtha* (तीर्थ, "holy bathing place"): A *samnyasi* who bathes with the feeling of truth in the *tirtha* of the triple confluence characterized by *tat*, *tvam*, and *asi*.

(2) *Ashrama* (आश्रम, "hermitage"): A *samnyasi* who is mature in accepting the [*samnyasa*] *ashrama*, completely devoid of the chains of desires, and completely free of birth and death.

(3) *Vana* (वन, "wood"): A *samnyasi* who dwells at a beautiful place desolate of people and is free from the chains of desires.

(4) *Aranya* (आरण्य, "related to a forest"): A *samnyasi* always located in a forest and living in bliss, leaving everything.

(5) *Giri* (गिरि, "hill"): A *samnyasi* whose eternal dwelling is on a hill, who is engrossed in the study of *Bhagavad Gita*, and whose resolve is deep and immovable.

(6) *Parvata* (पर्वत, "mountain"): A *samnyasi* who lives in the foothills, has advanced knowledge, and knows the worth and worthlessness [of everything].

(7) *Sagara* (सागर, "ocean"): A *samnyasi* who acquires the gem of deep knowledge from the ocean of truth and does not violate his moral bounds.

(8) *Sarasvati* (सरस्वती, "deity of speech"): A *samnyasi* who is ever engrossed in the knowledge of *svara* (OM or *Shabda Brahman*), expounds on *svara*, is the best of poets, and destroys

all that is worthless in the ocean of the world.

(9) *Bharati* (भारती, "knowledge"): A *samnyasi* who is replete with weight of knowledge, abandons all [worldy] onuses, and does not know (carry) the burden of grief.

(10) *Puri* (पुरी, "city"): A *samnyasi* who is full of essence of knowledge, situated in the state of the supreme essence, and engrossed in the Supreme Brahman.

As per the *Mathamnaya Setu*, Tirthas and Ashramas are associated with the Sharada (Dwarika) Matha; Vanas and Aranyas with the Govardhana Matha; Giris, Parvatas, and Sagaras with the Jyotish Matha; and Sarasvatis, Bharatis, and Puris with the Shringeri Matha.

Historically, the four *mathas* represented the highest organizational level of the *Dashanamis*. At the lowest level were *mathikas* (मठिका) ("small *mathas*"), which later came to be called *marhis* (मढ़ी) in Hindi. There are 52 *marhis* of the *Dashanamis* all over India. These *marhis* are members of the Shaiva *akharas* which represent the tradition of Adi Shankara at the Kumbha Melas.

The Jyotish Matha, Dwarika Matha, and Govardhana Matha are regularly represented by their respective Shankaracharyas at the Kumbha Mela. Swami Svarupananda Sarasvati (1924–2022), who held dual charge of the Jyotish and Dwarika Mathas, was often present at the Melas. Swami Nishchalananda Sarasvati (Puri Matha) is a regular visitor. The Shringeri Matha often has a symbolic presence at the Kumbha Mela. In 1977, Swami Abhinava Vidyatirtha (the then head of the Shringeri Peetha) and Swami Bharati Tirtha (the then successor-designate) had camped for a few days at the Prayaga Kumbha. They bathed at the Sangama on *Mauni*

Amavasya. In 2013, a small camp was set up by the Shringeri Peetha at the Prayaga Kumbha where around 60 students performed *sandhyavandana* and *svadhyaya* and chanted Vedic verses, Vishnu Sahasranama, and Lalita Sahasranama. Another prominent *Dashanami* to be present at recent Kumbha Melas was Jayendra Sarasvati (1935–2018), the former head of the Kanchi Matha. He participated in the Prayaga Kumbha Mela in 1989, 2001, and 2013.

Concluding Remarks

The world of sadhus at the Kumbha Mela is very diverse. There are sadhus wearing ochre robes, yellow robes, white robes, or nothing at all. There are the Shaiva *Dashanamis*, the Vaishnavas of many schools, the syncretic Udasinas, and the unique Nirmala Sikhs. There are *jagadgurus* who are embodiments of scriptural knowledge and who can speak extempore in poetic Sanskrit for hours. There are masters of hatha yoga who mesmerize onlookers with their command over postures. There are numerous silent sadhus engrossed in askesis in the extreme cold or extreme heat. There are sadhus displaying unbelievable physical feats of asceticism. There are Mahamandaleshvaras taking care of organizational issues. There are new initiates learning the ropes of the life of a sadhu. These myriads of sadhus are brought together by the *sangacchadhvam* spirit of the Kumbha Mela, the greatest unifier of the Hindu sadhus and Hindu faith.

5. *Kalpavasis* and *Tirthayatris*

At the Kumbha Mela, the asceticism of the tens of thousands of sadhus is complemented by the austerities of the lakhs of *kalpavasis* (at Prayaga) and the activities of the crores of *tirthayatris* (pilgrims). If the renunciate sadhus represent the tradition of *nivritti* (निवृत्ति, cessation from actions) at the Kumbha Mela, the worldly *tirthayatris* represent the tradition of *pravritti* (प्रवृत्ति, performance of actions), and the householder *kalpavasis* represent a stage between the two. Together, the sadhus, the *kalpavasis*, and the *tirthayatris* at the Kumbha Mela represent the balance of *nivritti* and *pravritti*.

Kalpavasis

The Sanskrit word *kalpa* (कल्प) refers to a period of 432 crore years, believed to be one day of Brahma. It also means a resolve or determination. The word *vāsa* (वास) means living or staying at a place. In the context of the Prayaga Kumbha Mela and the Magha Mela (also at Prayaga), *kalpavasa* refers to a vow observed by ordinary householders in which they stay on the banks of the Sangama for a long time (usually a month), leading a spartan and pious life. It is believed that *kalpavasa* in the month of *Magha* bestows the same merit as righteous acts performed for one full *kalpa*. Some Hindus believe that the word *kalpa* in *kalpavasa* is also associated with the concept of *kaya-kalpa* or rejuvenation.

Kalpavasa in Puranas

In the *Vishnu Purana*, the *Agni Purana*, and the *Shiva Purana*, the word *kalpavasi* is used for residents of the *Mahar-loka*, the fourth of the seven realms. The *kalpavasis* reside in *Mahar-loka* for one *kalpa* or a day of Brahma. In the *Bhagavata Purana* (4.9.21), the word *kalpavasi* is used for realms which last for a *kalpa*. In these examples the word is not used in the sense of somebody living in a sacred place for a long time.

The *kalpavasa* of the Kumbha Mela and the Magha Mela is most likely inspired by Puranic accounts like the *Magha-snana-vidhi* ("the ceremony of bathing in the *Magha* month") narrated by Dattatreya to Karttavirya in the *Magha-masa-mahatmya* ("greatness of the *Magha* month") section of the *Padma Purana*. Dattatreya tells Karttavirya (Sahasrarjuna) that when the Sun is in Capricorn in the month of *Magha*, a bath in a small puddle also results in even the sinners attaining *svarga*. Dattatreya says (refer the appendix for the original verses):

"I shall then narrate to you the supreme ceremony of bathing in the *Magha* month. A specific restraint in the form a vow is to be observed by the best of humans. For the sake of obtaining excessive fruit (merit), a wise person should give up eating something (a specific delicacy). One should sleep on the ground and offer sesame mixed with *ghee* [to the fire]. And one should worship Vishnu, the eternal Vasudeva, at three times. One should offer an *akhanda dipaka* (constantly burning lamp) for Madhava. O King, one should donate fuel, a blanket, clothes, footwear, saffron, *ghee*, oil, a cotton cloth, a pan or pot, cotton, a cotton cover, a cotton quilt, and grain as per one's ability in the month of *Magha*. One should give gold measuring one *rattika* (0.1215 grams) to a knower of the Veda. O king, that donation [in the month of *Magha*] is undecaying (of eternal merit) as the ocean. O king, one should not take heat from another's fire and give up accepting gifts. O king, at the end of *Magha* one should feed Brahmins as per one's ability and one desiring their welfare should give them *dakshina* (an offering)."

Dattatreya further says the following, which could be the possible reason behind the *kalpavasa* being called so, in the *Magha-snana-vidhi*—"O king, the sins that are accumulated by humans across many births for one *kalpa* are reduced to ashes for those who bathe in the bright and dark fortnights of the *Magha* month."

Kalpavasa in melas

Those who observe the *kalpavasa* in the Magha Mela and the Prayaga Kumbha Mela are called *kalpavasis*. They live a life of austerity with minimal comforts. While the *kalpavasis* come every year to Prayaga during the Magha Mela, their numbers are much higher when the Magha Mela becomes the Ardha Kumbha or Purna Kumbha (every twelve years). As per estimates, the 2013 Prayaga Kumbha had more than twenty lakh *kalpavasis*, up from around one lakh estimated by Deputy Inspector General (DIG) Trinath Mishra at the 1989 Prayaga Kumbha. They stayed in simple tents, *shiviras* of various saints and/or organizations, or even without a roof under the sky. In 2013, the Mela administration allotted 1,000 *bighas* of land apart from five sectors for the *kalpavasis*, who came from not only Uttar Pradesh but also from other states like Madhya Pradesh, Haryana, Delhi, Gujarat, and Punjab. Some foreigners also observed the *kalpavasa*, though most of them stayed in their respective gurus' tents. Around five lakh *kalpavasis* returned home after the penultimate *shahi snana* on 25 February 2013, the *Maghi Purnima* day.

The *kalpavasis* are perhaps the most faithful pilgrims of the Prayaga Kumbha Mela. Most of them are not formally affiliated to any of the *akharas*. They are not a part of the entourage of any religious or spiritual leader or organization, traditional or modern. They are not the focus of most documentaries on Kumbha Mela nor do they figure prominently in coffee table books. And yet, they are present in large numbers at every Magha Mela and Prayaga Kumbha Mela, silently undergoing their vows while residing in simple and small tents, eating once a day, bathing thrice a day, and finding bliss in meditating, chanting, reading, listening, and singing.

The *kalpavasis* are mostly *grihasthas* (householders, literally "staying in a house"). Traditionally, married couples observe the *kalpavasa* together though widowers and widows are allowed to observe it alone. In some senses, the *kalpavasa* is similar to the *Vanaprastha*, the third *ashrama* (stage) of life in ancient India. The *kalpavasis* leave their families and children behind during the *kalpavasa*. Many *kalpavasis* are middle-aged or old (in their seventies or even eighties).

Local residents of Prayagraj also observe the *kalpavasa*. An example is Chandarakala Devi, who attended her fifth Kumbha as a *kalpavasi* in 2013. She was a witness to the stampede of the 1954 Kumbha which killed hundreds and injured thousands. In all the five Kumbha Melas from 1954 to 2013, she lived on the banks of the Sangama during the Mela. In the past, many influential and affluent residents of Prayagraj have also observed the *kalpavasa*. Mark Tully wrote about Vibhav Bhushan Upadhyay, the former Advocate General of Uttar Pradesh who spent a full month away from his large house in Prayagraj living as a *kalpavasi* during the 1989 Mela.

The rules of *kalpavasa* include eating uncooked food (fruits and milk) or simple cooked food once a day, fasting on all main festivals, bathing thrice a day, performing *sandhyavandana* all three times, sleeping on the ground, observing self-restraint, staying in *brahmacharya* (abstinence), chanting mantras, and keeping good company (*satsanga*). In addition, according to Swami Nishchalananda Sarasvati, the *kalpavasis* are supposed to cook their own food; live a solemn and simple life; bathe in the Ganga early morning (in the *brahma muhurta*); avoid laziness, laughter, worldly matters, and loose talk; and engage in chanting (*japa*), askesis (*tapas*), and self-restraint (*samyama*).

Shayya Dana

After observing 12 *kalpavasas*, a *kalpavasi* performs what is called *Shayya Dana* (शय्या दान). *Shayya Dana* literally means "donating one's bed" but all worldly belongings including furniture, utensils, clothes, jewellery, and even electronic gadgets can be donated. Some people donate even gold during *Shayya Dana*. *Shayya Dana* symbolizes much more than a mere donation. In a way, the *Shayya Dana* is like performing one's own last rites. Couples usually do not observe *kalpavasa* any more after they have performed *Shayya Dana*. Many couples perform *Shayya Dana* before they become too old to observe the vows of the *kalpavasa*.

It may come as a surprise to the modern reader that even in the materialism of the twenty-first century, countless *kalpavasis* uphold the values of austerity and charity and perform *Shayya Dana* after twelve *kalpavasas*. All four grandparents of Richa

Pandey, an officer in the Stamps and Registration Department of Uttar Pradesh, performed twelve *kalpavasas* in late 1990s and 2000s from *Makara Sankranti* to *Vasanta Panchami*. Her paternal grandparents, Sadananda Pandey and Kamala Devi Pandey from Pratapgarh, performed *Shayya Dana* in 2010, while her maternal grandparents, Ishvara Chandra Tripathi and Pali Devi Tripathi from Prayagraj, performed *Shayya Dana* at the 2001 Prayaga Kumbha. Richa recalls visiting them during their *kalpavasa* camps in 2001. They consumed both uncooked food (fruits, milk, and curd) and cooked food—simple rice and dal—prepared using *chulhas* (चूल्हा, earthen or brick stoves) running on *upalas* (dried cow dung cakes). They would bathe twice at the Sangama every day and perform *arati* in the evening after their bath. They would spend the cold nights without any heating, sleeping on beds made of straw (*pual*). Their only source of light would be Petromax lamps and a street light provided by the Mela administration. During the day, they would listen to *kathas*, sing bhajans (devotional songs), and perform *kirtana* (repeating the divine name). While the Pandeys camped close to the Sangama, the Tripathis had to walk quite some distance to the Sangama for their baths. At the time of their *Shayya Dana* in 2010, the Pandeys got a cot (*charpai*) constructed and donated it to a pandit along with bedding.

Dates of *kalpavasa*

There is a difference of opinion on when the month-long *kalpavasa* is to be observed at Prayaga. Some *kalpavasis* observe the *kalpavasa* from the eleventh day of the bright half of *Pausha* to the twelfth day of the bright half of *Magha*, some others start it from the new moon day or the full moon day when the Sun is in Capricorn, and some others observe it from *Makara Sankranti* to *Vasanta Panchami*. In either of the three cases, the *kalpavasis* leave the Mela several days before the *Maha Shivaratri*, which is when the sadhus leave after the last *shahi snana* at Prayaga.

Kalpavasa at other Kumbhas

The *kalpavasa* is observed every year during the Magha Mela in addition to the Ardha Kumbha and the Purna Kumbha Melas at Prayaga. People also observe *kalpavasa* at the Kumbha and Ardha Kumbha Melas in Haridwar, albeit in much smaller numbers. The *kalpavasa* tradition is not popular at the Kumbha Melas in Ujjain and Nashik-Tryambakeshwar.

The *kalpavasi* President

Dr. Rajendra Prasad, the first president of independent India, was a man with deep respect for the traditions and culture of India. While being the first citizen of the country, he performed three *kalpavasas* on the banks of the Sangama, starting in 1952. Many leaders including Prime Minister Jawaharlal Nehru and Lal Bahadur Shastri would come and meet him at Prayaga during his *kalpavasa*. At his *kalpavasa* during the 1954 Kumbha, he stayed at Akbar's fort near the Sangama. Large crowds of people would gather to get a glimpse of their President. The place where the President stayed was later named "President's viewpoint" from where the entire Kumbha Nagari was visible. Unfortunately, a section of the media criticized his presence after the stampede on the *Mauni Amavasya* day in 1954, saying that the police administration was busy with ensuring that the President bathed in the Sangama while ignoring the masses which led to the stampede. The President visited the hospital in the Kumbha Nagari to visit the injured and issued a statement condoling the deaths.

Kalpavasis and immunity

In February 2013, during the Prayaga Kumbha, a team of thirty Indian researchers conducted a study on the *kalpavasis*. They concluded that the *kalpavasis* at the Kumbha Mela are quieter and more relaxed than an average person. In addition, the study concluded that *kalpavasis* develop stronger immunity towards diseases and that the life-style of the *kalpavasa* including bathing in the Sangama is akin to natural immunization. The study also mentioned the presence of bacteriophages in the waters of the Ganga.

The last finding was not new. As early as in the 1890s, the English bacteriologist Ernest Hankin had observed that the water of the Ganga had something special against *Vibrio cholerae*, the bacteria that cause cholera (called *vishuchika* in Sanskrit) in humans. Hankin noted that cholera was relatively 'tame' on the banks of the Ganga despite people leaving dead bodies in the river waters. New outbreaks of cholera on the banks of the Ganga did not spread like an epidemic (as would happen close to water supplies in Europe), rather they subsided fairly quickly and died out. Hankin observed that while filtered Ganga water retained the antibacterial effect, boiled Ganga water was not that effective. He concluded that the source of the antibacterial property of Ganga water could pass through a fine porcelain filter. At the beginning of the twentieth century, the French-Canadian microbiologist Félix d'Herelle discovered bacteriophages, the viruses that infect bacteria. Since then, it has been suggested that the waters of the Ganga contain phages which prevent the rapid spreading of cholera despite millions taking bath in the river.

In 2016, Krishna Khairnar of the National Environmental Engineering Research Institute (NEERI) published an article in the Journal of Biological Research (Thessaloniki) on the presence of bacteriophages at the origin of the Ganga (Gomukh). Further research is expected to throw more light on this anti-bacterial property of Ganga water. In the same year, Heather Hendrickson of Massey University in New Zealand told BBC Future's World-Changing Ideas Summit in Sydney that the bacteriophages on the banks of Ganga need to be reconsidered to deal with antibiotic-resistant bacteria which claim around a few hundred thousand lives each year.

The *kalpavasis* at the Magha Mela and the Prayaga Kumbha Mela who bathe in the Ganga every day provide an opportunity for such medical research that may benefit humanity. I am reminded of the words of Tulasidasa—"Only that fame, that poetry, and that prosperity is good which benefits all, like the river Ganga." If the Kumbha Mela, the greatest festival of humanity, can help solve some medical problems for the benefit of humanity, it would only bring to fruition the prayer of India's seers: *sarve bhavantu sukhinaḥ sarve santu nirāmayāḥ, sarve bhadrāṇi paśyantu mā kaścid-duḥkha-bhāg-bhavet*, which translates as "May all be pleased, may all be healthy, may all see (experience) prosperity, may none experience sorrow."

Tirthayatris

The Sanskrit word *tīrtha* (तीर्थ) for a sacred place comes from the root √*tṝ* (तॄ) ("to swim across") and literally means "a means of going across [sins or the worldly ocean]". The word *yātrā* (यात्रा), from the root √*yā* (या) ("to go"), means "journey" or "the act of going". Therefore, *tīrthayātrā* (तीर्थयात्रा) refers to pilgrimage and a *tīrthayātrī* (तीर्थयात्री) is somebody who takes up a pilgrimage, i.e. a pilgrim. While technically anybody who travels to the Kumbha Mela is a *tirthayatri*, the word mostly refers to an ordinary pilgrim as opposed to a sadhu or saint. In this chapter, I use the term *tirthayatri* to refer to pilgrims at the Mela who are neither sadhus nor *kalpavasis*. These *tirthayatris* make up the majority of the participants at the Kumbha Mela today.

A microcosm of India

The Kumbha Mela attracts devout Hindus from almost all parts of India (and Nepal). Captain Raper wrote in 1808 that the Haridwar Kumbha was "attended by people from all parts of Hindustan and the Dekhin (Deccan)". Mark Tully wrote of the 1989 Prayaga Kumbha that people had "flocked from the north, the south, the east, and the west". Prayaga being the *tirtharaja*, *tirthayatris* at the Prayaga Kumbha come from the most diverse geographies in India and Nepal. The microcosm of India that one finds at Prayaga during the Kumbha is even more fascinating than that seen in Varanasi, a city called *tirtharaji* ("having a line of *tirthas*") like Prayaga is called *tirtharaja*.

While a majority of the participants at the Prayaga Kumbha are from North India, the Mela has attracted South Indians also for a long time. The Hindi poet Suryakant Tripathi Nirala wrote of a South Indian in the 1930s who had come from the then Madras Presidency to take a bath at the Prayaga Kumbha. The participation of the Shringeri Shankaracharya Swami Abhinava Vidyatirtha in the 1977 Prayaga Kumbha has been mentioned in chapter 4. D. P. Dubey and Miroslav Krása have written about the practice of widows and South Indian women who had their heads shaved entirely at the 1989 Prayaga Kumbha, in contrast to other married women who had only a symbological little piece of hair shaved. Despite these references, Mark Tully noted at the 1989 Prayaga Kumbha that "only the south of India seemed to be thinly represented". I believe there are several reasons for the underrepresentation of South Indians at the Prayaga Kumbha. Firstly, *akharas* of armed sadhus have not historically had a strong presence in the South. The long distance between Southern states and Prayaga is another factor—till 1989, most pilgrims arrived at the Kumbha Mela on foot. A third reason is the presence of similar festivals in the South like the Mahamaham and the Pushkaram. There may be some other possible reasons, for example C. N. Venugopal writes that Lingayats, who form around 20% of Karnataka's population, do not participate in the Kumbha Mela. The under-representation of the South seems to be changing in the twenty-first century. There were several firsts at the 2013 Prayaga Kumbha—the Tirumala Tirupati Devasthanams (TTD) set up a replica of Lord Venkateswara's *vigraha*, Mata Amritanandamayi of Kerala participated in the Mela, and Bhakthi TV (a 24/7 Telugu devotional channel) broadcast programmes on the Kumbha Mela every day. I have personally interacted with several South Indians who visited the Kumbha Mela at Prayaga in 2001 or 2013 without any history of elders in their family doing it. An example is Indavara Gayathri, who comes from a Smarta Brahmin family in Bangalore. She attended her first Kumbha Mela at 2013 in Prayaga. She loved the experience so much that she attended the 2016 Kumbha at Ujjain also and was back in Prayaga for the 2019 Ardha Kumbha, where a large number of South Indians participated.

The other Kumbha Melas have historically been more localized in comparison to the Prayaga Kumbha. Till the end of the last century, the *tirthayatris* at the Haridwar Kumbha used to be mostly from northern and eastern India, those at the Ujjain Kumbha mostly from central India, and those at the Nashik-Tryambakeshwar Kumbha mostly from western India. This is changing rapidly in the twenty-first century as people travel more and more for pilgrimages. Chaitanya Deshpande and Sumita Sarkar wrote of the many tourists from Punjab, Rajasthan, Uttar Pradesh, Madhya Pradesh, and South India at the 2015 Nashik-Tryambakeshwar Kumbha. A group of 30 members of Kabui Dharma Sabha came from as far as Manipur to offer prayers and meet gurus at the Nashik Kumbha.

Demographics

In a study published in August 2018 in *Prabandhan: Indian Journal of Management* as part of *The Kumbha Mela Experiment*, Ashish Verma and two other researchers studied the demographics of pilgrims at the 2016 Ujjain Kumbha. Based on a survey of more than 2,500 *tirthayatris* at the Mela, the authors reported that the largest number of visitors was in the 18–25 years range followed by that in the 35–45 years range. This contrasts with the *kalpavasis* at Prayaga who are mostly married couples in sixties and seventies. Around 60% of the respondents were males and almost 65% were married. More than half of those surveyed belonged to a family with 5–8 members, around 45% were either graduates or post-graduates, and nearly 23% were employed with a government or private organization as opposed to 22% who were self-employed. Around 27% of the respondents were students and 26% were housewives. More than 60% of the respondents were from the low-income group, earning less than Rs 10,000 per month. Finally, an overwhelming majority (94%) of the respondents said they were satisfied with their life. Some of these findings are confirmed by my experience from the melas at Prayaga, Nashik, and Ujjain where I observed that families from the lower and lower-middle income groups constituted the majority of the *tirthayatris*.

Motivation

Traditionally, faith has been the major motivation behind the *tirthayatris* visiting the Kumbha Mela. At the 1989 Prayaga Kumbha, when M. Darrol Bryant asked Ram Sharma—who had walked fifteen days from Bihar to be a part of the Mela—why he had come, Sharma had simply said, "To bathe in the Ganga." Like Sharma, crores of *tirthayatris* over the ages have been primarily motivated by their unshakeable faith in India's sacred rivers and her sadhus and saints.

This seems to be changing in the twenty-first century as the Kumbha Mela becomes more Indian and more global. In addition to their demographics, Verma et al. also studied the motivation of the *tirthayatris* behind visiting the 2016 Ujjain Kumbha. They arrived at the following interesting conclusions, using logistic regression techniques. While old-aged *tirthayatris* were majorly motivated by the opportunity to exchange intellectual ideas and visit saints, the young *tirthayatris* were motivated by the opportunity to see a once-in-a-lifetime event. Males were more motivated by the prospect of visiting saints, while females were more motivated by the opportunity to be away from home with their families. Respondents from low-income group, mostly daily wage earners, were motivated by a desire to find meaning in life or to meet people with similar interests, while private employees were motivated by the chance to see a once-in-a-lifetime event. The researchers concluded that looking for new experience was the biggest motivation factor across all demographics and that people who were happy in their lives tended to show a higher gratitude to God by participating in the Kumbha Mela.

Charaiveti, charaiveti

From bathing in the sacred rivers to visiting various temples to hearing *kathas* to having meals to exploring the Mela, most *tirthayatris* travel on foot at the Kumbha Mela. In a study published in *Sustainable Cities and Society* in July 2018 as part of *The Kumbha Mela Experiment,* Ashish Verma and four other researchers presented results of analysing walking data of 2,510 *tirthayatris* at the 2016 Ujjain Kumbha. The data was collected with the help of local volunteers equipped with small GPS units. Verma et al. found that the mean distance the *tirthayatris* covered by walking at the Kumbha Mela was 1.75 km, much higher than the mean walking distance for similar studies for other mass gathering events. The authors concluded that the *tirthayatris* were willing to walk for more than 20 minutes to offer prayers, to bathe in the river, and to visit their *shiviras*. They were willing to walk much less for drinking water or eating food and the least for shopping. The authors found that the young (18–25 years old) and the old (> 45 years old) walked more than the middle-aged (25–45 years old), the young possibly due to better fitness and the old possibly due to higher motivation. Based on their analysis of acceptable walking distances and times, Verma et al. recommended that mass transport facilities be provided up to around 1 km away from the bathing area and drinking water and food stalls be provided within radii of 655 m and 450 m, respectively, from the river banks.

United by Hindi

One hears many languages being spoken at the Kumbha Mela among various groups of *tirthayatris*. I have heard Hindi, Bhojpuri, Awadhi, Gujarati, Marathi, Bengali, and Telugu at the Kumbha Melas in Prayaga, Nashik, and Ujjain. Speakers of different languages from different regions of India freely and comfortably use Hindi as the common link language. Sadhus from various parts of the country also use Hindi as their link language and most discourses are held in Hindi to appeal to a wider audience at the Mela. If there are any doubts about Hindi being the *de facto* national language of India, a visit to any of the Kumbha Melas would put them to rest. This is true not only of the Kumbha Melas at Prayaga, Haridwar, and Ujjain (held in Hindi-speaking states), but also of the Nashik-Tryambakeshwar Kumbha in Maharashtra: Hindi was spoken and understood widely in Nashik at the 2015 Mela.

Concluding Remarks

In some respects, the *kalpavasis* and *tirthayatris* are very different from each other. The *kalpavasis* are present in lakhs at the Prayaga Kumbha while the *tirthayatris* are present in crores at all the four Kumbha Melas. While the *kalpavasis* are mostly old couples, the young account for the largest group among the *tirthayatris*. The *kalpavasis* leave behind their families while the *tirthayatris* mostly travel with their families. The *kalpavasis* stay for one full month spending a lot of time on their internal journey at the Kumbha Mela, while most *tirthayatris* come to the Mela for a few days spending a lot of time on their external journey to and from the Mela. The life of the *kalpavasis* at the Kumbha Mela is quiet and spartan, while that of the *tirthayatris* is vibrant and colourful. Despite these disparate differences, the *kalpavasis* and the *tirthayatris* are ordinary householders united by their faith and brought together by the *saṅgacchadhvam* spirit of the Kumbha Mela.

6. New-age Hindu Movements

The sadhus and their *akharas*, the *kalpavasis*, and the *tirthayatris* have been present at Kumbha Melas for a long time. In addition, a host of popular new-age Hindu movements have increasingly participated in Kumbha Melas recently. These movements differ greatly in their beliefs and practices from the traditional Hindus and Hindu organizations—some are vehemently opposed to certain traditional Hindu practices, some proselytize with a missionary zeal, some are run professionally like multinational firms, and some are exclusively popular among urban Indian and/or foreigners. Despite these differences, the participation of these new-age movements in the Kumbha Mela is no less enthusiastic. In this chapter, I cover some such new-age Hindu movements and organizations and their participation in the Kumbha Mela. This is not an exhaustive coverage and there are many more similar active participants in the Kumbha Mela. It is heartening to see these new-age movements and organizations do a lot of charitable work, including feeding and/or treating the *tirthayatris* for free, in a traditional Hindu gathering.

Arya Samaja

The Arya Samaja, founded by Dayananda Sarasvati in 1875, is still active in many parts of India. At the 1855 Haridwar Kumbha, its founder Dayananda Sarasvati had raised a disruptive flag called the *Pakhanda Khandini Pataka* ("the flag to refute hypocrisy"). During the late nineteenth century and well into the twentieth century, there was a fierce ideological war between the Arya Samajis and traditional Hindus (called *Sanatanis*). The Arya Samaja has not seen the success many thought it would in the last century. Today, the war is no longer as fierce—the Arya Samaja is not as strong as it once was while the Hinduism of Sanatanis continues to be more popular.

The Arya Samaja has a small presence at the modern Kumbha Melas. The Uttar Pradesh Arya Pratinidhi Sabha set up a *Vaidika Dharma Prachara Shivira* at the 2013 Prayaga Kumbha in sector 9 of the Kumbha Nagari. The *shivira* ran from 3 January to 25 February. At the 2016 Ujjain Kumbha, the Madhya Bharata Arya Pratinidhi Sabha set up a *shivira* which had a *yajna-shala*, a book stall for distribution of books, and informative exhibitions. The Samaja invited Vedic scholars, bhajan singers, musicians, and brahmacharinis (girl students of Vedic texts) to be a part of the *shivira*. In the 2019 Ardha Kumbha at Prayaga, the Arya Samaja set up a small *shivira* in sector 19 of the Mela area. Outside the *shivira* hung a banner which read *Pakhanda Khandini Pataka*.

Scholars of the Arya Samaja have historically campaigned against Puranic beliefs, *jyotisha*, *tirthayatra*, *shraddha*, *murti-puja*, etc. In the run-up to the 2016 Ujjain Kumbha, however, Dr. Vivek Arya of the Samaja focussed on countering Christian missionaries who he said may try to take advantage of the Kumbha Mela to convert Hindus. Dr. Arya made several suggestions to pre-empt this, including propagation of Vedic literature at the Kumbha Mela and resolving all disputes among *akharas* over *shahi snana* in advance.

Transcendental Meditation Movement

The Transcendental Meditation (TM) Movement was started by Mahesh Yogi (known to his followers as Maharishi). In addition to teaching the TM techniques, the Maharishi group of organizations promotes study of Vedic texts and Ayurveda and runs several universities.

The Maharishi group of organizations has been well-represented at the Kumbha Mela for a long time. Mahesh Yogi flew to India to be a part of the 1960 Haridwar Kumbha, where he was greeted by the Shankaracharya of Jyotish Matha and the President of India, Dr. Rajendra Prasad. He held a TM camp from 2 to 15 April at the Mela. Mark Tully wrote about the notable presence of the TM group at the 1989 Prayaga Kumbha. Dr. Tony Nader, head of the Global Country of World Peace, and his Cabinet Ministers travelled to India to attend the 2001 Prayaga Kumbha. The TM movement has continued its participation in the Kumbha Mela even after Mahesh Yogi passed away in 2008. In 2013, around 1,000 delegates (including Dr. Tony Nader) of the Maharishi movement from 120 countries camped at the Prayaga Kumbha. The *Maharishi Samadhi Smaraka*, a large memorial dedicated to Mahesh Yogi, was inaugurated during the Mela. At the 2016 Ujjain Kumbha, the Maharishi Veda Vijnana Vishva Vidyapeetham set up a large Maharshi Shivira. One of the major attractions of the *shivira* was the *Atirudrabhisheka Mahayajna* where hundreds of Vedic pandits performed the *Rudrabhisheka* every day by chanting the *chamakam* and *namakam* hymns from the Yajur Veda. In addition, *kathas* on *Shiva Purana* and *Bhagavata Purana* were organized at the *shivira*.

ISKCON

The International Society for Krishna Consciousness (ISKCON) or the Hare Krishna movement was founded by Bhaktivedanta Swami in 1966. The missionary zeal with which its followers, many foreigners and urban Indians, propagate their faith makes it very different from followers of traditional Hindu *sampradaya*s and other Gaudiya Vaishnava institutions.

ISKCON participates regularly at the Kumbha Mela on a large scale. Its founder Srila Prabhupada himself visited the 1977 Prayaga Kumbha along with his followers. The Hare Krishnas believe, as the *Chaitanya Charitamrita* says, that Chaitanya Mahaprabhu had once stayed at Prayaga during the month of *Magha* and bathed at the Sangama for ten days. Like in the case of the TM movement, ISKCON continued to participate in the Kumbha Mela after Srila Prabhupada passed away in November 1977.

At the 2010 Haridwar Kumbha, ISKCON's *shivira* had a 20-foot-high diorama of Chaitanya Mahaprabhu. Its kitchen fed around 15,000 people every day. The *shivira* had around 600 devotees staying. At the 2013 Prayaga Kumbha, there *shivira* provided accommodation for 1,000 people. The *shivira* had dioramas depicting various Puranic episodes and the kitchen distributed free *prasada* to 5,000 people every day. ISKCON volunteers took out processions, distributed books for free, and chanted the Hare Krishna mantra. At the 2015 Nashik-Tryambakeshwar Kumbha, the ISKCON *shivira* had a medical clinic to treat people for free in addition to a kitchen. At the 2016 Ujjain Kumbha, ISKCON's *shivira* in Mangalanatha Zone had a hemispherical screen in a dome-shaped auditorium with a seating capacity of one hundred. The auditorium showed a film on the Puranic account of the *samudra manthana* ("churning of the ocean"). Daily programmes at the *shivira* included discourses on the *Bhagavata Purana* and a bullock-cart *yatra* with the chanting of the Hare Krishna mantra.

At the 2013 Prayaga Kumbha, I witnessed a rather disruptive act by some ISKCON followers. They gathered a retinue of 15–20 impoverished children, most likely given some allurement, and entered the premises of other *shivira*s one by one, chanting mantras and slogans hailing their founder on a handheld loudspeaker. Many organizations hold such processions in the public space at the Mela, but this invasion of space allotted to other *shivira*s was different. More than anything, it reflected a domineering and imposing attitude that one associates with proselytizing movements like ISKCON.

Swaminarayan Sanstha

The Bochasanwasi Shri Akshar Purushottam Swaminarayan Sanstha (BAPS) is an offshoot of the Vadtal Gadi of the Swaminarayan Sampradaya. It has many followers in Gujarat and among the Gujarati diaspora around the world. Established in 1907, BAPS has grown quite influential over the past few decades. Today it runs more than 700 temples and 3,300 centres, including the magnificent Akshardham temple in New Delhi. Like ISKCON, BAPS is multinational, affluent, and influential. Unlike ISKCON, it does not actively proselytize.

As per the *Nilakantha Charitra*, Sahajanand Swami (also called Swaminarayana), the founder of the Swaminarayana Sampradaya, visited the Kumbha Melas of Haridwar and

Kumbakonam as a teenager. Despite this, the BAPS has not had a very notable presence at the Kumbha Melas. This is slowly changing. On 30 July 2003, just three days after the Nashik-Tryambakeshwar Kumbha Mela started, BAPS inaugurated a new Swaminarayan Mandir in Nashik. BAPS volunteers set up an *anna kshetra* ("food area") which served free breakfast, lunch, and dinner to sadhus and *tirthayatris* during the Mela and fed more than 90,000 people from 30 July to 3 September. The volunteers also served free tea, coffee, and snacks on the *shahi snana* days. A team of doctors and paramedical staff of BAPS Medical Services set up a mobile dispensary in the mandir and treated around 35,000 *tirthayatris* free of charge. An exhibition on deaddiction was set up to emphasize the benefits of quitting tobacco, *gutkha*, smoking, and alcohol. Several senior Swamis of BAPS took part in the *shahi snana*s on behalf of Pramukha Swami Maharaja. At the 2015 Nashik-Tryambakeshwar Kumbha also, a team of 300 BAPS volunteers set up an *anna kshetra*, a medical camp, and a deaddiction exhibition at the BAPS mandir. Perhaps for the first time, 180 BAPS sadhus visited the Kumbha Mela, worshipped the Godavari, and participated in a special bath. Nearly 300 BAPS volunteers offered services for the entire duration of the Mela. For the 2025 Kumbha, Prime Minister Narendra Modi has requested every foreign branch of the Swaminarayan movement to get one hundred visitors to the Mela.

The Art of Living

The Art of Living (AOL) is an international educational and humanitarian organization founded by Sri Sri Ravi Shankar in

1981. It is headquartered outside Bangalore and operates in more than 150 countries. AOL is run quite professionally. Many of its volunteers like Vikram Hazra (singer, writer, and AOL's program director who was formerly a journalist at Economic Times) come from a professional background.

AOL has had a regular presence at the Kumbha Mela for quite some time. Sri Sri Ravi Shankar participated in the 2010 Haridwar Kumbha in Haridwar and also celebrated Holi at the Mela with some prominent sadhus like Baba Ramdev and Chidananda Muni. At the 2013 Prayaga Kumbha, AOL set up an exquisite *shivira* in sector 8 of the Kumbha Nagari. Sri Sri Ravi Shankar visited the Mela for three days in February, and personally met with many saints including Avadheshananda Giri (Juna Akhara), Nishchalananda Sarasvati (Govardhana Peetha), Chidananda Sarasvati (Paramartha Niketana), and Swami Ramabhadracharya (Tulasi Peetha). At the AOL *shivira*, meditation, *Rudrapuja*, and *satsanga* programmes were held. AOL also organized a festival for the youth called the *Yuvotsav* at the Mela on 12 February.

Patanjali Yogapeeth

The Patanjali Yogapeeth was founded by Baba Ramdev and Acharya Balkrishna in 2006 at Haridwar. It is owned by the Divya Yog Mandir Trust. Today, it is one of the largest and the most influential religio-spiritual organizations in India. The success story of Patanjali Yogapeeth and its sister organization Patanjali Ayurveda (a Rs 12,000 crore FMCG company) is nothing less than phenomenal.

The organization has had a regular presence at the Kumbha

Melas where it promotes Yoga and Ayurveda. At the 2013 Prayaga Kumbha, Baba Ramdev arrived with a large entourage of followers on 2 February. For seven days, from 3 to 9 February, he taught hatha yoga and pranayama exercises every morning from 5 am to 7.30 am at the Guru Karshni Shivira in sector 12. At the 2015 Nashik-Tryambakeshwar Kumbha, a seven-day Yoga Shivira was conducted by Baba Ramdev from 19 to 23 September, again at the Guru Karshni Shivira. It was inaugurated by Swami Sharanananda, Avadheshananda Giri, and Swami Jnanananda along with Baba Ramdev. At the 2016 Ujjain Kumbha, Baba Ramdev taught *kriyas* of hatha yoga to thousands of attendees every morning at the Prabhu Premi Sangha Shivira, where Avadheshananda Giri delivered a *katha* on the *Bhagavata Purana* in the afternoon. Avadheshananda Giri performed hatha yoga in Baba Ramdev's session and the latter also sat to hear the *katha* delivered by the former. Baba Ramdev also organized a *kavi sammelana* ("gathering of poets") at the 2016 Ujjain Kumbha.

Paramartha Niketana

The *Paramartha Niketana Ashram* was established by Swami Shukadevananda in 1942 at Rishikesh. It is one of the largest ashrams at Rishikesh. From 1986, it has been led by Swami Chidananda Sarasvati (also known as Chidananda Muni), who is respected by traditional *akharas* and also popular among foreigners. The renowned daily Ganga Arati performed by Chidananda Muni at the ashram has attracted many dignitaries. He is also the founder of the Ganga Action Parivar (GAP), an organization of scientists, activists, spiritual leaders, and volunteers dedicated to preservation and protection of the Ganga and its tributaries.

Chidananda Muni attends most Kumbha Melas and is known for taking up novel initiatives like "Green Kumbha" at the 2013 Prayaga Kumbha. This first-of-its kind programme was carried out in partnership with NGOs, educational institutes, and government ministries. As part of the programme, Chidananda Muni not only campaigned for planting trees, prohibiting plastic, and cleaning trash but also set an example by cleaning the banks of the Sangama with his disciples on several occasions. Chidananda Muni was involved in perhaps the most diverse set of activities over two months at the Mela. Some of these were:

(1) yoga, pranayama, and meditation sessions by Iyengar Yoga teachers and Baba Ramdev

(2) yajnas on special occasions like *Makara Sankranti*

(3) meeting with and/or hosting many notable saints, industrialists, researchers, journalists, political leaders, and Bollywood personalities

(4) many social awareness events like Green Pilgrimage Conference, Ganga Sansad, National Day of the Girl Child, and Republic Day Environmental Parade

(5) a procession of 5,000 school children to spread the message of saving rivers

(6) cultural events like poetry and music programmes

(7) devotional events like *bhajan sandhyas*

(8) Sangama Arati with leaders of several religions and a Maha Sangama Arati with many Hindu leaders

(9) large *bhandaras* feeding up to 5,000 sadhus

(10) a mass wedding of 150 poor couples

(11) conferences on Ayurveda, yoga, vegetarianism, and spirituality

The range of these programmes and the diversity of people and organizations Chidananda Muni worked with at the 2013 Prayaga Kumbha is overwhelming. This is a great example of the *sangacchadhvam* spirit of Kumbha, where diverse people come together and work towards a common goal.

Brahma Kumaris

The Brahma Kumaris movement was started by Lekhraj Kriplani in the 1930s as *OM Mandali*. Today, the Brahma Kumaris World Spiritual University (BKWSU) has more than 8,000 centres in more than 110 countries. Its headquarters are at Mount Abu in Rajasthan. Right from its foundation, the movement has been largely led by women.

The Brahma Kumaris often deliver a social message through their presence at the Kumbha Mela, drawing attention to crimes against women and emphasizing the need of women empowerment. At the 2013 Prayaga Kumbha, the BKWSU set up a unique exhibition where girl students dressed as the Hindu goddesses Durga, Sarasvati, Vaishno Devi, Shitala, Kali, and Parvati; despite the Brahma Kumaris movement not believing in *saguna* Brahman. At the 2016 Ujjain Kumbha, BKWSU set up a *shivira* called the Satyam Shivam Sundaram Adhyatmika Mela. It had a 40-feet-high exhibition of Hindu goddesses, replicas of the twelve *jyotirlingas*, an exhibition with automated dioramas on spiritual themes and a depiction of the *samudra manthana*, a 4-D laser show, hologram shows, a model of an ideal village, and a room for meditation. The *shivira* organized several interactive programmes including *rajayoga* sessions and spiritual discourses.

All World Gayatri Pariwar

The All World Gayatri Pariwar (AWGP) was founded by Pandit Shrirama Sharma Acharya and is currently led by Dr. Pranav Pandya. Headquartered at its Shantikunja ashram in Haridwar, AWGP runs more than 5,000 centres, including many temples called *Gayatri Shaktipeethas*, across the world.

AWGP is involved with the Kumbha Melas in several ways. Its large Shantikunja ashram offered free boarding facilities and food to *tirthayatris* during the 2010 Haridwar Kumbha on a first-come-first-served basis. At the same Mela, a convention titled "Nationwide Tobacco Control for Mass Awareness" was organized by AWGP to address the social issue of drug addiction. In addition to religious and spiritual leaders, medical experts like Dr. Rakesh Thakur (cancer specialist at the All India Institute for Medical Sciences), Uttarakhand Health Director Dr. Asha Mathru, and the Kumbha Mela Officer on Special Duty (OSD) Dr. Anil Sharma attended the convention.

At the 2016 Ujjain Kumbha, AWGP organized *yajna*s with 108 *kunda*s and Puranic *katha* programmes every day. In addition, AWGP organized multiple nine-day *Sanjivani Sadhana Yajna*s. In each such *yajna*, 108 AWGP members chanted the Gayatri Mantra 24,000 times while offering *ahuti*s to the fire. AWGP set up a large book stall and offered many of their publications, worth Rs 1 crore, at half price during the entire duration of the Mela. Dr. Pandya was one of the chief guests at the inauguration of the *Antarrashtriya Vichar Mahakumbha* (see chapter 7) on 12 May at the Mela.

Concluding Remarks

Followers of many new-age Hindu religious and spiritual movements and/or organizations actively participate in the Kumbha Melas. The sadhus with their traditional *akhara*s and *sampradayas*, the *kalpavasis*, and the *tirthayatris* can be considered the traditional participants at the Kumbha Mela, in contrast to these modern participants. The followers of these modern Hindu movements at the Kumbha Mela differ in many respects from traditional Hindus. This, however, does not prevent them from participating enthusiastically in the Kumbha Mela, a traditional Hindu event. This is another way how the *saṅgacchadhvam* spirit of the Kumbha Mela brings tradition and modernity together, making the Mela traditionally modern.

Rainbow on earth: Colourful tents of pilgrims during the Prayaga Kumbha. Image © UP Tourism

The ephemeral city that never sleeps: Kumbha Nagari of Prayaga during the night. Image © UP Tourism

Nobody goes hungry: A *bhandara* at the Prayaga Kumbha with free food for all. Image © UP Tourism

Centre of focus: A camera focuses on an indifferent sadhu at the Prayaga Kumbha. Image © UP Tourism

A mela for all: An Indian guru with his foreign disciples at the Prayaga Kumbha. Image © UP Tourism

Solitude in the crowd: Two women praying at the Prayaga Kumbha. Image © UP Tourism

Defeating the cold: Pilgrims bathing early morning at the Prayaga Kumbha. Image © UP Tourism

To and fro: Pilgrims crossing the floating pontoon bridges at the Prayaga Kumbha. Image © UP Tourism

Arghya for *arka*: A pilgrim offers water to Surya (the sun) at the Prayaga Kumbha. Image © UP Tourism

Praying to the mother: A woman offers a lamp to Ganga at the Prayaga Kumbha. Image © UP Tourism

The march of sadhus: Vaishnava sadhus crossing a pontoon bridge at the Prayaga Kumbha. Image © UP Tourism

A glimpse of South India: *Kodai* (cloth umbrella), *thombai*s (cloth pillars), and *aalavattam* (cloth shield) at the Prayaga Kumbha. Image © UP Tourism

Embodiments of *Shakti*: A procession of *sadhvis* (women sadhus) at the Prayaga Kumbha. Image © UP Tourism

Chhatrapatis: A royal procession of Vaishnava sadhus at the Prayaga Kumbha. Image © UP Tourism

Natural living: Huts of straw at the Prayaga Kumbha.
Image © Shutterstock (ravi090)

The city of lights: Kumbha Nagari seen from a distance during the Prayaga Kumbha. Image © Shutterstock (pratyush085p)

Mane show: A sadhu with his long *jatas* overshadowing his horse's mane at the Prayaga Kumbha. Image © Sudhanshu Kesarwani

Hair it is: A Naga sadhus shows his matted hair at the Prayaga Kumbha. Image © Sudhanshu Kesarwani

Photo finish: Naga sadhus reach the Sangama waters at the Prayaga Kumbha. Image © Sudhanshu Kesarwani

Most diverse, most inclusive: Foreign women at the Prayaga Kumbha. Image © Sudhanshu Kesarwani

Chai pe charcha: Three sadhus meeting at the Prayaga Kumbha. Image © Sudhanshu Kesarwani

A bare beginning: Initiation of new Naga sadhus at the Prayaga Kumbha. Image © Sudhanshu Kesarwani

Royal sight: People gather to have a glimpse of sadhus at the Prayaga Kumbha. Image © Sudhanshu Kesarwani

Winter warmth: People meeting each other during the night at the Prayaga Kumbha. Image © Sudhanshu Kesarwani

7. Literature, Arts, and Music

Hinduism is one religion which has embraced literary arts, fine arts, and performing arts as no other. One cannot imagine Vedic Hinduism without the sublime hymns like the *Shiva Sankalpa Sukta*, the mathematically artistic *yajnavedis*, and the mellifluous melodies of the Sama Veda. Itihasic and Puranic Hinduism without the *Sundara-kanda* of Valmiki's Ramayana, the Natarajas of the Chola era, and the *gitas* (songs) of the *Bhagavata Purana* would be a dull lake without any flowers or birds. Folk Hinduism is also rich in literary, artistic, and musical traditions. At the Kumbha Mela, the largest Hindu gathering, one finds a *triveni sangama* (triple confluence) of literature, arts, and music. This chapter focusses on how literature, arts, and music are closely intertwined with religious and spiritual activities at the Kumbha Melas, making them as much cultural melas as religious.

Printed Literature

The Gita Press, a nearly 100-year-old publication house based in Gorakhpur, had sold nearly 66.5 crore books as of July 2018. Despite a labour crisis that hit Gita Press in September 2015 (when its sales stood at 58 crore books), it has continued to flourish. The low-cost, flawless, and very well-produced books published by Gita Press have contributed a lot towards spreading and preserving Hinduism. It should not come as a surprise to the reader that the maximum contribution towards sales of Gita Press books comes from the Magha Melas and the Kumbha Melas held at Prayaga. The *tirthayatris* who come to Prayaga during the melas buy religious books considering them to be *prasada* of Prayaga. Being good-quality and yet low-cost, Gita Press books are in high demand, especially among the lakhs of *kalpavasis* who read and recite religious texts during their stay at the Kumbha Mela. At other Kumbha Melas too, the Gita Press puts up book-stalls—they had a large stall with many titles at the 2016 Ujjain Kumbha.

Hundreds of other organizations set up stalls at the Kumbha Mela to sell books. The AWGP offered books worth Rs 1 crore for sale at half price at the 2016 Ujjain Kumbha. Some organizations distribute books for free. ISKCON volunteers distributed 3,800 copies of the *Bhagavad Gita* on the first day of the 2013 Prayaga Kumbha. The 2003 issue of the annual publication *Varshiki* by the Central Hindi Directorate reported that 50 lakh religious books were sold during the 2003 Nashik-Tryambakeshwar Kumbha. The numbers would have been much higher for Prayaga Kumbha. Along with the attendance at the Kumbha Melas, India's literacy rate has also increased tremendously since 1947, leading to a higher demand of books at the Kumbha Mela as booksellers in Haridwar noticed in 2010. India's literacy rate grew from 18.33% in 1951 to 74.04% in 2011 (four-fold increase), while that of Uttar Pradesh grew from 12.02% to 69.72% (a nearly six-fold increase) in the same period. The attendance at 2013 Prayaga Kumbha was more than twenty times that at the 1954 Prayaga Kumbha, but the attendance of literate people in 2013 would have been nearly one hundred times that in 1954.

New literature is also composed at the Kumbha Mela which sees the participation of many erudite sadhus and saints. Swami Ramabhadracharya authored the *Raghavakripabhashyam* (राघव-कृपाभाष्यम्) series of Sanskrit commentaries on the *Brahma Sutra*, the *Bhagavad Gita*, and major Upanishads during the 1998 Haridwar Kumbha. He has authored many other works during his stays at Kumbha Melas, for example the *Bhringadutam* (भृ-ङ्गदूतम्), a Sanskrit *dutakavya* ("messenger-poem"), was mostly composed during the 2004 Ujjain Kumbha.

Lastly, literature on the Kumbha Mela is also a unique contribution of the Kumbha Mela to literature. Experiences at the Kumbha Mela are often captured in books on the Kumbha Mela; some of these experiences are very valuable. Dr. Trinath Mishra, a 1965 Indian Police Service (IPS) officer, was the Senior Superintendent of Police (SSP) of Prayagraj during the 1977 Kumbha Mela. He studied the notes left by his predecessors and wrote a Hindi book by the name *Kumbha Gatha* which was published in 1989 and was on sale during the 1989 Prayaga Kumbha, when he was the DIG of Prayagraj range. At the 1989 Kumbha, photographer David Osborn and 'Surfing Swami' Jack Hebner spent seven weeks living in a tent, photographed until they ran out of film, and later published the book "Kumbha Mela: The World's Largest Act of Faith". Indian Administrative Service (IAS) officer Jai Shankar Mishra was the secretary of Urban Development, Government of Uttar Pradesh, during the 2001 Prayaga Kumbha. To a great extent, he was responsible for the successful conduct of the 2001 Kumbha, which the BBC called "the greatest show on earth till date". Three years later, he published a book titled "Mahakumbh, the Greatest Show on Earth" in which he shared many details which went into organizing the 2001 Kumbha Mela. A detailed study of the 2013 Prayaga Kumbha from the perspective of mass gathering event management was published by a team of the Bihar State Disaster Management Authority (BSDMA).

Oral Literary Tradition

Hinduism has a rich history of oral tradition, where learning is passed on from the guru to the *shishya* orally as opposed to writing. The adjective *well-read* is used in English for a person who is very knowledgeable and learned, as a result of having read a lot. I am not aware of an equivalent word in Sanskrit. However, Sanskrit has a unique word whose English equivalent I am unaware of—*bahushruta* (बहुश्रुत). The word is used for a knowledgeable and learned person, but literally means "one who has heard a lot". The implication is that in the Indian literary tradition, a lot of learning is acquired not by reading but by listening to the guru. This is reflected in the abundant *samvadas* that are present in Puranas and *Itihasas*.

The oral tradition is still alive in India as far as religious and spiritual learning goes. The Kumbha Mela is a vibrant platform where knowledge and skills are transferred through oral traditions, as India's nomination to the UNESCO rightly noted. Kapil Kapoor, a scholar of linguistics and literature and former Rector (Pro-Vice-Chancellor) of the Jawaharlal Nehru University (JNU), attributes his learning of the *Mahabharata* to the many *kathas* he heard sitting in different pandals as a child during the Kumbha Melas. He believes that the tradition of *kathas* and *pravachanas* helps in transferring rich knowledge in a democratic way through a vernacular medium.

Uncountable *shiviras* have *katha* or *pravachana* programmes organized throughout the Kumbha Mela. Most programmes are in Hindi or another Indian language and are based on themes found in *Itihasas* and Puranas (e.g. *Valmiki Ramayana*, *Bhagavata Purana*, and *Shiva Purana*), philosophical texts (e.g. *Bhagavad Gita*, Upanishads, and *Brahma Sutra*), or vernacular devotional texts (e.g. *Ramacharitamanasa* and *Bhaktamala*).

The crest-jewel of the oral tradition of India is the tradition of Vedic chanting, which is also on UNESCO's Representative List of Intangible Cultural Heritage of Humanity. Many traditional and modern organizations have pandits reciting Vedic hymns during the Kumbha Mela. Some organize grand *Rudrabhisheka* programmes where tens of Vedic pandits together recite the *chamakam* or *namakam* verses from memory. Others have smaller *havanas* with pandits reciting beautiful Vedic hymns like the *Purusha Sukta* and the *Shiva Sankalpa Sukta*. Many such programs involve young students from a *Veda Pathashala*. At the 2013 Prayaga Kumbha, 62 students of the *Bharati Tirtha Veda Pathashala* in Prayaga (run by the Shringeri Sharada Peetha) chanted hymns from the *Madhyandina* (Shukla Yajur Veda), *Kauthuma* (Sama Veda), and *Shaunaka* (Atharva Veda) *shakhas* every day for three hours, from 9 am to 12 noon.

Occasionally, *kavi sammelanas* ("meetings of poets") are also organized. At the 2016 Ujjain Kumbha, one such *sammelana* was organized by Baba Ramdev at the Shri Karshni Kumbha Mela Shivira. A similar meet was organized by Baba Ramdev at the Shri Karshni Kumbha Mela Shivira in the 2019 Ardha Kumbha at Prayaga also. It is noteworthy that the Sanskrit words *sammelana* and *mela* come from the same root.

Arts

The Kumbha Nagari houses thousands of temporary pandals during the Mela. Many a pandal has an artistic design, much like the temporary pandals put up during Ganeshotsava in Mumbai or Durga Puja in Kolkata. The pandals of many affluent new-age organizations like AOL, ISKCON, and TM movement have a distinctly aesthetic look. Some traditional sadhus and organizations also have very artistic pandals. At the 2016 Ujjain Kumbha, the pandal of Nishchalananda Sarasvati had a sober yet elegant entrance with an all-saffron cloth background and an all-white low-relief foreground which comprised text in an attractive typeface, a statue of Shankaracharya, arches, borders, and a ceiling medallion. The pandal of Bholanath Giri, an *urdhvabahu* Mahant of the Avahana Akhara, was modelled after a Rajput palace with magnificent *chhatris* (pavilions with canopies), intricate *jalis*, and artistic arches and pillars. The pandal housed a 121-feet-long *agarabatti* (incense stick) made from *kandas* (dried cow-dung cakes), *havana* ingredients, and Ayurvedic herbs. In addition, there was an enormous statue of Shiva and a 108-feet-long *trishula* (trident of Shiva). Skilled artisans from Gujarat camped and worked for one full month at Ujjain to complete work on the pandal, which cost Rs 1 crore to make. Although rich and grand, the pandal was like any other pandal in other respects: it ran a large *anna kshetra* to distribute free food to *tirthayatris* all day and organized a three-day *Kamadhenu Mahayajna* for *goraksha* ("protection of cows").

At the 2015 Mela, a majestic gate was constructed by the Nashik Municipal Corporation at the entrance of the *sadhugrama* in Nashik on Nashik-Aurangabad highway. The design of the permanent structure depicted the confluence of the cultures of Vaishnavism and Maharashtra. The gate had 14 carved concrete pillars (seven on either side). Five concrete arches with 25 saffron triangular flags above them and 14 hanging bells below them joined the ten central pillars. The unmissable structure, named *Jagadguru Ramanandacharya Pravesha-dvara*, was constructed at the cost of more than one crore rupees. Every time I passed it, I was awed by its size and aesthetics.

Art exhibitions have also been held at the Kumbha Mela for quite some time. Hardev Sahai, a former freedom fighter and *gosevaka* from Haryana, organized a large exhibition with around 25,000 paintings and posters on the theme of *goraksha* at the 1954 Prayaga Kumbha. ISKCON's camp at the 2013 Prayaga Kumbha had thirty life-size motor control dioramas depicting various Puranic themes. The 2016 Ujjain Kumbha had an exhibition of paintings and sculptures made by differently-abled students of the Jagadguru Ramabhadracharya Vikalanga Vishvavidyalaya. The exhibition was visited by the Chief Minister Shivraj Singh Chouhan. Some amateur painters also paint in public view at the Mela.

Martial arts are often displayed by sadhus at the Kumbha Melas. During their processions, many Naga sadhus display their fighting skills using sticks or swords, sometimes solo and sometimes in a mock-fight with another sadhu. Such displays of martial arts are one of the last remnants of the time when sadhus fought with weapons against Islamic militants, the East India Company (during the Sannyasi Revolt), and occasionally with sadhus of other *akharas* at Kumbha Melas.

Music

Music is an integral part of everyday life at the Kumbha—so much so that M. Darrol Bryant wrote that the noise at the 1989 Prayaga Kumbha was "a veritable cacophony of words, music and mantras". In my experience of four Kumbha Melas, what appears to be a cacophony is in fact multiple parallel musical euphonies coming together. The word for music in Sanskrit is *sangita* (सङ्गीत), which as per Indian musicological texts includes singing (*gita*), playing of an instrument (*vadya*), and dancing (*nritya*) all three. This section covers all three aspects of *sangita* in the context of Kumbha Melas.

Singing

Sadhus, especially Vaishnavas, have had a centuries-old tradition of music in northern India. The sixteenth century mystic Swami Haridasa, who founded the *Sakhi Sampradaya* as an offshoot of the Nimbarka tradition, made significant contributions to Hindustani music. *Sakhi Sampradaya* sadhus are now a part of the Radhavallabhi Nirmohi Akhara, a sub-group of the Nirmohi Akhara, which participates in the Kumbha Melas. The *sakhis* spend their day at the Mela singing songs devoted to Krishna and dancing in front of other sadhus. Many other Vaishnava sadhus can be seen playing the *ektara* and singing the *Ramdhun* interspersed with verses from the *Ramacharitamanasa*.

Outside of the world of sadhus, thousands of folk and semi-classical or classical singers come to the Kumbha Mela as part of a *Rama Lila* or *Krishna Lila* troupe or a musical group travelling with a *katha-vyasa* who holds *katha* programmes.

In addition, many *katha* artistes are themselves good singers. *Katha* programmes often start with a *kirtana* which involves repeatedly singing names of Rama, Krishna, or Vishnu. The *katha* audience joins the *katha* artiste and stage singers during the *kirtana*. The countless bhajan *mandalis* singing bhajans in small groups with harmonium and cymbals and the *kalpavasis* singing verses from religious texts add to this large motley crew of singers at the Kumbha Mela. At the 2016 Ujjain Kumbha, many folk song genres like Birha, Bundeli, and Khol Sankirtan were showcased as part of the month-long *Simhastha Kala Utsava*. The Kumbha Mela is a delight for musicophiles who can experience numerous forms of folk and popular Indian music at one place.

Musical instruments

Various types of drums and other instruments are played by large bands on special occasions at the Kumbha Mela like the *peshwai* and flag-hoisting of *akharas* as well as during the march of the sadhus towards the river on the day of a *shahi snana*. The beats of the drums add to the energy and vibrancy of the Kumbha Mela. The dhol (ढोल) is a slightly large drum which is usually hung around the neck or the shoulder and played with sticks. It is a common sight in religious and family celebrations in many parts of India. In Maharashtra, bands of dhol players, known as *dhol pathak*s (ढोल पथक), are very popular. During the 2015 Nashik Kumbha, several *dhol pathaks* had hundreds of members including many young girls and boys, doctors, engineers, and even a district judge. The *damaru* (डमरु), literally "that which makes a *dam* sound", is a small drum held and played with one hand. Many Naga sadhus carry and play *damaru*s at the Kumbha Mela. The *damaru* has long been associated with ascetics: it was used by *kapali* yogis, who carried a human skull, during the middle ages. The *damaru* is also the instrument of Shiva, called *damaru-hasta* ("having a *damaru* in hand") in the *Skanda Purana*. It is believed that the fourteen *Shiva Sutra*s of Sanskrit grammar originated when Shiva played his *dhakka*, an old form of *damaru*, at the end of his dance. Musicians like Pt. Chhannulal Mishra believe that all the *talas* of Hindustani music originate from the *Shiva Sutras*.

Another common instrument at the Kumbha Mela is the *shankha* (शङ्ख), or the conch shell. *Tirthayatris* blowing the *shankha* while bathing in the river is a common sight. The blowing of *shankha* dates back to the Vedic times. In the *Madhyandina Samhita* of the Shukla Yajur Veda, a blower of *shankha* is called *shankhadhma*. *Shankha* is the deity of a hymn in the Atharva Veda and is held in the hand by Vishnu and Mahakali as per Puranas.

Most *katha* programmes at the Mela are accompanied by harmonium and *tabla* performers. Every day, harmonium and *tabla* players enliven the mood of hundreds of *kathas* at the Mela. During my visit to the 2016 Ujjain Kumbha, I shared a rickshaw ride with two such performers. They told me that they were in Ujjain for the entire duration of the Mela would be performing at their camp thrice every day.

Many other small instruments like the *ektara*, the *dapha*, the *dholak*, the *khartal*, the *chimta*, and the *manjira* are used by bhajan *mandalis* at Kumbha Melas. The *shehnai* appears to have been used in the past during *akhara* processions but I have not observed its use in recent times.

Dance

Like singing and playing of instruments, dancing is also common to both sadhus and non-sadhus at the Kumbha Mela. In 1989, Tully observed naked sadhus dancing with abandon, "twirling wooden staves like demented drum majors" at the Prayaga Kumbha. Even today, the Shaiva Nagas are known to break into an impromptu dance to the beats of dhols during the *peshwai* of their *akhara* or as they are marching towards the river for the royal bath. The dances of Vaishnava sadhus from the *Sakhi Sampradaya* have already been mentioned. Sometimes the dance is limited to whirling in a trance; some Vaishnava sadhus at the Mela perform such dances with closed eyes, balancing a *kalasha* on their head at the same time.

Given its pan-India attraction, the Kumbha Mela has rightly been used as a stage for the display of folk music and dance forms from across India in recent times. During the 2010 Kumbha Mela in Haridwar, a *Swar Ganga* ("Ganga of musical notes") programme was organized in which the cultural heritage of India was presented on one stage. The programme saw a full house with many people standing outside the pandal. Folk dancers from Assam, Gujarat, Kashmir, Maharashtra, Manipur, Rajasthan, Uttarakhand, and Uttar Pradesh performed at the programme. Martial arts from Gujarat, Kerala, and Manipur were displayed. Narendra Singh Negi showcased the best of Garhwali music while Hema Malini presented her famous Shiva-Shakti ballet.

Dance performances by artiste troupes are a part of the numerous *Rama Lila* and *Krishna Lila* programmes popular at the Prayaga Kumbha. These programmes were usually staged in the evening at the 2013 Prayaga Kumbha. Solo folk dancers performing the *Mayura Nritya* ("peacock dance") of Vrindavan can be spotted in the crowd from their peacock feathers. Performers of Lezim, a Maharashtrian folk dance, were a part of the tableau procession during the flag-hoisting ceremony in Nashik at the 2015 Nashik-Tryambakeshwar Kumbha.

A month long *Simhastha Kala Utsava* was organized by Madhya Pradesh's Department of Culture in collaboration with the Ministry of Culture of Government of India at the 2016 Ujjain Kumbha. More than 3,000 artistes were invited from various states to present song, music, and dance performances at five stages—named after Bharata Muni, Vikramaditya, Bhoja, Kalidasa, and Bhartrihari—during the month-long *Kala Utsava*. In addition to popular dance and dance-drama forms like Odissi, Kathak, Mohiniattam, *Rama Lila*, and *Krishna Lila*, many not-so-popular folk and tribal dance forms were showcased at Bhoja Mancha. These included Seraikella Chau and Paika (Jharkhand), Lalilang (Assam), Gotipua (Odisha), Chhattisgarh Nacha (Chhattisgarh), Dandiya (Gujarat), and Balan Nacha (popular with Nepali tribes in Darjeeling and Sikkim). On 8 May, the eve of the second *shahi snana*, a dance-drama on creation in Santhali by a 15-member troupe of Santhal tribals from Jharkhand left the audience enraptured. From 12 to 14 May, a three-day programme was held in which tribal dance artistes from Chhota Udepur and the Panchmahals showcased Gujarat's tribal culture through their dances. The Bharat Baria-led troupe was invited by Pilot Baba, a popular sadhu and a regular at Kumbha Melas who served as a Wing Commander in the Indian Air Force before becoming a sadhu.

A Kumbha of Thoughts

A new experiment was carried out at the 2016 Ujjain Kumbha in which a three-day event called the *Antarrashtriya Vichar Mahakumbha* ("the international great Kumbha of thoughts") was organized at Ninora, near Ujjain, from 12 to 14 May when the Mela was in progress. The event covered not only religious topics but also social topics from the fields of agriculture, environment, education, culture, language, health, cleanliness, and empowerment of women. The high-profile event was attended by several dignitaries including Sri Lankan president Maithripala Sirisena, Indian Prime Minister Narendra Modi, Lok Sabha speaker Sumitra Mahajan, Chief Ministers of many Indian states, and RSS Sarsanghchalak Mohan Bhagwat among others. Participants included religious leaders like Avadheshananda Giri and Chidananda Muni, United Nations Women representative Anju Pandey, academics like Jay O' Keeffe and Subhash Kak, social workers like Nivedita Bhide, and scholars like Dayananda Bhargava and David Frawley. Lawmakers from Bangladesh, Bhutan, Malaysia, Nepal, and Sri Lanka were also invited to the event. The event was a novel initiative and can serve as an example for Kumbha Mela organizers in the future.

Concluding Remarks

In his *Nitishataka*, the poet-philosopher Bhartrihari says:

"One (a human) who is devoid of literature, music, and arts is a veritable animal, [albeit] without tail and horns. That he lives on without eating [their] fodder is the highest good fortune for animals."

What Bhartrihari suggests is that it is literature, music, and arts that refine humans and set them apart from animals. Hindu religion and practices are inseparable from these human traditions of classical and folk literature, music, and arts in India. All these three human traditions are brought together by the *saṅgacchadhvam* spirit of the Kumbha Mela, the largest celebration of humanity.

8. Commerce and Technology

Commerce and technology are getting increasingly interconnected in India. In May 2024, then Union Minister Rajeev Chandrashekhar reported that India's digital economy, which was around 4.5% of India's GDP in 2014, had become 12% of the GDP in 2024 and was expected to become 20% of the GDP by 2026–27. Information technology (IT) and IT enabled services (ITeS), Electronics, Telecom, and E-commerce are the major components of India's digital economy.

The Kumbha Mela has been a platform for commercial and trade activities for centuries. Modern technology has been present at the Mela since the times of the British Raj. The Mela continues to benefit from commerce and technology in the twenty-first century. In fact, the Kumbha Mela of today is unimaginable without modern commerce and modern technology. In this chapter, I focus on the commercial and technological aspects of the Kumbha Mela which are often not covered in depth in books on the Kumbha Mela.

Commerce

Trade: Then and Now

Captain Francis Raper gave a vivid account of the trade at the 1808 Haridwar Kumbha. He wrote about the presence of merchants from Punjab, Kashmir, and even Kabul at the Mela. Animals including horses, mules, camels, and cattle were sold at the Mela. Other items that were available for sale included spices, dry fruits, garments, brassware, ivory, and toys. Over two centuries, while the trading of animals has almost disappeared, sale of many other items has grown. One of them is printed literature. As mentioned in the previous chapter, an estimated 50 lakh books were sold during the 2003 Nashik-Tryambakeshwar Kumbha. Booksellers at Haridwar also reported a marked increase in demand for books at the 2010 Mela.

Spending and revenue

For a long time, the Kumbha Mela has been a source of revenue for successive governments. During the British rule of India, revenue obtained from the Prayaga Kumbha would be used to update medical, health, and sanitation facilities as well as to increase salaries and maintain buildings in Prayagraj. As per records kept in the Regional Archive Office (RAO) of Prayagraj, the British government rewarded the Mela manager and inspector with Rs 150 from the revenue received from the 1870 Prayaga Kumbha. The records state that in 1906, the revenue from Prayaga Kumbha for the government was around Rs 10,000 while the budget for Mela management was around Rs 30,000. Some media accounts state that in 1882 the cost of organizing the Kumbha Mela was Rs 20,228 while the revenue was Rs 49,840, with a net profit of Rs 29,612. Amit Agnihotri, the Regional Archives Officer of Prayagraj in 2013, said that the revenue during the melas seemed to come from maximum utilization of resources and licensing.

All four Kumbha Melas have seen a massive increase in government spending in the last two decades as they have grown in scale. The organization of the Mela now involves a government spending of several thousand crore rupees. In 1989, the Uttar Pradesh government spent around Rs 12 crore (USD 8 million) for organization of the Prayaga Kumbha. The government budget grew to Rs 120 crore (USD 26 million) for the 2001 Kumbha. It further grew to Rs 1,000 crore (USD 183 million) in 2013—3.7 times the 2001 budget adjusting for inflation. The estimated budget for the 2025 Mela at Prayaga is Rs 6,382 crore. In 2010, the Uttarakhand government spent Rs 600 crore on organizing the Haridwar Kumbha. The lion's share of the funds was contributed by the centre. In 2004, the Madhya Pradesh government spent Rs 262 crore on the Ujjain Kumbha and its revenue was projected to be around Rs 10 crore. In 2016, the government budget grew massively to Rs 5,000 crore. The Maharashtra government spent Rs 2,500 crore on the 2015 Nashik-Tryambakeshwar Kumbha.

While statistics on government spending on the various melas are available, those for revenue from the melas are not easy to get. The Associated Chambers of Commerce and Industry of India (ASSOCHAM) had predicted before the 2013 Prayaga Kumbha that the Mela would generate a revenue of Rs 12,000 crore for the government, including Rs 1,500 crore for Uttar Pradesh Tourism and Railways. In 2015, ASSOCHAM estimated that the Nashik-Tryambakeshwar Kumbha would generate a revenue of Rs 10,000 crore for the Maharashtra government. In 2016, Ravindra Pastor, the Divisional Commissioner of Ujjain, told *Business Standard* that the Ujjain Kumbha Mela was a Rs 11,000 crore floating economy. As per media reports, the 2025 Kumbha Mela is expected to generate a revenue of Rs 25,000 crore.

Job creation

The ASSOCHAM report before the 2013 Prayaga Kumbha predicted that 6.35 lakh new jobs would be created by the Mela, split across the informal sector (55,000), the hotel industry (2.5 lakh), airlines and airports (1.5 lakh), tour and travel services (45,000), and eco-tourism and medical tourism (50,000). ASSOCHAM estimated before the 2015 Nashik-Tryambakeshwar Kumbha that the Mela would generate 4.5 lakh new jobs. The report said that the Mela would generate direct and indirect opportunities in every key segment which touches a large number of people.

Informal sector

The informal (unorganized) sector, estimated to employ around 80% of India's workforce, sees large business during the Kumbha Mela, as evinced by the ASSOCHAM job creation estimates above. The Kumbha Mela greatly benefits people in the informal sector including tailors, cobblers, porters, mechanics, tea vendors, street vendors, rickshaw drivers, cab drivers, boatmen, etc. Not only is the Kumbha Mela an economic booster for the informal sector, the Mela offers those working in the sector a great learning opportunity. An example of this was on display in the Saregama Shakti documentary on the 2010 Haridwar Kumbha, in which a tea vendor spoke on camera about how he knew tea preferences of *tirthayatris* from different states of the country.

Hospitality

The hospitality sector sees a boom during the Ardha and Purna Kumbha Melas. At the 2010 Haridwar Kumbha, hotels were fully booked for the entire three-month duration of the Mela more than three months in advance. In addition to 34 major ashrams and 50 major hotels, many smaller ashrams, hotels, and *dharmashalas* were available for stay. The options ranged from simple lodgings where guests could cook their own food to five-star comforts with fine dining. The Shantikunja Ashram of AWGP offered free stay and food to everybody on a first-come-first-served basis. The Prem Nagar Ashram offered 600 rooms and expected up to one lakh people staying over three months. Baba Ramdev's Patanjali Yog Peeth offered more than 1,000 rooms ranging from Rs 50 per bed per day in the dormitory to Rs 1,100 per bed for a three-bed AC room. At the other end of the spectrum was Haveli Hari Ganga, a Heritage hotel located at Ram Ghat, which offered rooms at Rs 6,000 per day without any liquor or non-vegetarian food.

The story is similar at the other Kumbha Melas. Around 200 small and big hotels offered 3,500 rooms during the 2015 Nashik-Tryambakeshwar Kumbha. The ASSOCHAM report that came out before the Mela predicted that the hotel industry would see 100% occupancy during the Mela as opposed to 55–60% on average.

Involvement of corporates

At the 2013 Prayaga Kumbha, Tata Chemicals (a part of the Tata Group) collaborated with the Uttar Pradesh Jal Nigam for providing free drinking water to *tirthayatris*. Tata Chemicals produces Tata Swach, a water purifier indigenously developed at Pune's Tata Innovation Centre and first launched in 2009. Under the Tata Swach banner, Tata Chemicals set up 28 kiosks with 300 water purifiers. Each kiosk was manned by staff to help *tirthayatris*. During the Mela, the kiosks served around 5 lakh litres of drinking water to around 20 lakh pilgrims. Ashvini Hiran, the Chief Operating Officer (COO) of consumer products division at Tata Chemicals, said that this effort was their "small contribution to this mammoth congregation of humanity" and that they were happy that their "tie-up with the UP Jal Nigam Board in this public-private partnership initiative was fruitful". This public-private partnership, another example of the *saṅgacchadhvam* spirit of Kumbha, is an example to emulate for Mela administrators and corporates.

Some corporates have come up with novel advertizing strategies at the Kumbha Melas that help the *tirthayatris* in addition to promoting a brand. At the 2013 Prayaga Kumbha, the telecommunications services provider Idea sponsored the display boards which had the helpline numbers of police control room, fire service, and ambulance service. Ogilvy came up with an intelligent advertizing strategy for Unilever at the Mela. Unilever partnered with more than 100 dhaba owners in the vicinity of the Kumbha Nagari. For every food order placed with the dhabas, the first roti was stamped with the message "*Lifebuoy se haath dhoye kya?*" ("Did you wash hands with Lifebuoy?") in Devanagari using a heat stamp. Unilever ran this campaign for thirty days starting from 1 February. In addition, Unilever placed Lifebuoy soap in the washrooms of all dhabas and used banners and billboards at the dhabas. Unilever estimated that around 25 lakh rotis were stamped with their message, which suggests around 800 rotis were stamped at every dhaba in a day.

Reckitt Benckiser went several steps ahead of Unilever at the 2015 Nashik-Tryambakeshwar Kumbha. It used radio, leaflets, and public announcements to emphasize the importance of washing hands before eating. The firm deployed 100 hand-wash agents on the ground who distributed around 66,000 Dettol hand sanitizer packs for free. In addition, around 100 low water consumption pumps were installed by the firm in Nashik. The firm claimed its campaign resulted in sixty-seven lakh hands being washed and thirty lakh litres of water being saved, though the numbers appear to be exaggerations. The free distribution of hand sanitizers and creation of awareness were good examples of corporate social responsibility (CSR) initiatives which firms can take during the Kumbha Mela. Reckitt Benckiser was rightly commended by the Maharashtra Chief Minister for its awareness campaign at the Mela. However, one aspects of Reckitt Benckiser's campaign after the Kumbha was highly irresponsible—a video highlighting the campaign on Dettol India's YouTube channel stated that the 2015 Nashik Kumbha was truly a 'Dettol ka dhula' Kumbha Mela. Such brazen appropriation of the Kumbha Mela, which truly belongs to the sadhus and *tirthayatris*, is reprehensible and must be avoided by corporates at all costs.

Technology

Crowd management

Crowd management is a big challenge at the Kumbha Mela. As technology has proved to be immensely helpful for this purpose, Mela organizers have increased their dependence on technology with time. It started with the 2001 Prayaga Kumbha when big-screens were put up at a distance of 20 km from the Sangama to help the *tirthayatris* plan their entry into the Kumbha Nagari. The increasing use of CCTV cameras for security and crowd management at the Kumbha Mela has already been mentioned in chapter 3. A satellite-census of the Mela crowds was conducted in 2010 by three satellites (Cartosat-I, Cartosat-II and IRS Liss-4) which captured high-resolution photographs of the congregation on the last *shahi snana* day (14 April) at the Haridwar Kumbha. At the 2013 Prayaga Kumbha, there was GPS mapping of all sectors in Kumbha Nagari and traffic police installed electronic signboards on major roads to ease traffic and to display information. The police used CCTV cameras to continuously monitor crowds on the 12-feet-wide pontoon bridges on the busiest days. Police personnel in the control room, led by the Inspector General (IG) Alok Sharma, zoomed in on any bridge as soon as it appeared to be overcrowded. If they concluded it was indeed overcrowded, they instantly relayed this information to the police personnel on the ground who would then divert the crowd to other bridges to balance the load. Sharma told Diego Buñuel of the National Geographic that it was crucial to keep the crowds moving, even if they were being sent the wrong way, as stopping the crowds would amount to hara-kiri. Sharma meant that suddenly stopping the continuous flow of people could lead to a rumour which could potentially cause a stampede. The use of technology in Kumbha Nagari certainly helped—there was no stampede in the Kumbha Nagari at the 2013 Mela, the biggest Kumbha Mela to date. Unfortunately, a stampede occurred on the *Mauni Amavasya* day at the Prayagraj railway station, 5 km from the Kumbha Nagari.

Reuniting lost people

An ingenious use of technology helped the administration achieve something incredible during the 2015 Kumbha Mela at Nashik-Tryambakeshwar. Each of the nearly 2,500 people who went missing in the Mela was reunited with their family or friends. A control room was set up by the administration in partnership with NGOs like Bharat Bharati. Its helpline number was widely publicized on posters and banners put all over the Mela area by Nashik police. Besides using CCTV cameras and public announcement systems, the administration also engaged as many as 160 volunteers who between them could speak sixteen languages and communicate with each other using a mobile application. The mobile application was developed by Tata Consultancy Services (TCS). It helped Bharat Bharati share photos of missing persons with the volunteers. Two missing people were located with the help of the application. This network of volunteers complemented nearly 24,000 Nashik police personnel, who mostly knew only Marathi and Hindi, deployed in the Mela area. Every time a missing person case was reported, announcements were made on PA systems all along the Mela area in the language the lost person understood. This achievement of the administration at Nashik Kumbha was hailed by several media outlets. However, some Indian elites remained incorrigible as ever and hailed the achievement in their own way. A report on a mainstream news website reported the story with the headline "Sorry, Bollywood; People Aren't Going Missing at Kumbh Mela Any More", reducing a major achievement to a loss of a stereotyped plot for Bollywood.

Kumbhathon

Kumbhathon, a brainchild of the Massachusetts Institute of Technology (MIT) Media Lab, was a notable technology initiative at the 2015 Nashik-Tryambakeshwar Kumbha. Led by Ramesh Raskar (associate professor at MIT Media Lab) and backed by Ratan Tata (chairman emeritus of Tata Sons), the initiative brought together scientists, engineers, students, social workers, and officials to develop technology solutions for improving the Kumbha Mela experience through technology start-ups. There were five Kumbhathon camps at the Mela which held workshops and seminars. The Kumbhathon helped develop several real-time applications:

(1) The official Kumbha App: an application for *tirthayatris* which provided news and information on crowds, transport, availability of parking and hotels, and temples.

(2) Crowd Steering: an application for Mela administrators to monitor and redirect crowds using heatmaps.

(3) Medi Tracker: an information system about medical facilities and navigation to ambulances and health centres.

(4) Annadan: an application for managing donated food.

(5) ASHIOTO: a rubber doormat to count and report footfalls for crowd control. It was developed by Nashik's 15-year-old Nilay Kulkarni in partnership with three engineers.

(6) Epimetrics: a system for monitoring health.

(7) Naksha: a smartphone-friendly digital map.

A 'Wiki takes Nashik' project was launched as part of the Kumbhathon in which over 100 college students from Nashik worked on uploading 5,000 pictures of Nashik under 18 categories (including geography, history, mythology, arts and culture, agriculture, people, industry and tourism) on

Wikimedia Commons. It was a novel approach to improve the Wikipedia page on Nashik by involving local tech-savvy youth.

Technology at 2016 Ujjain Kumbha

At the 2016 Ujjain Kumbha, Bharat Sanchar Nigam Limited (BNSL) laid 100 km of optical fibre cables and equipment to provide 73 wireless hotspots. The district administration and Mela organizers developed a mobile application for providing information on bath days, facilities, and emergency services at the Mela. Online bookings were accepted for the *bhasma arati* at the Mahakaleshvara temple. An Indore-based company was assigned the responsibility of running 350 battery-operated e-rickshaws during the Mela. After the end of the Mela, 100 e-rickshaws were allowed to ply on the main roads of Ujjain.

While the Kumbhathon in 2015 was driven by the MIT Media Lab, technology start-ups were officially involved in 2016 at Ujjain. The district administration invited online tenders for technology solutions to improve the experience of the Kumbha. A parking solution was provided by the Delhi-based start-up getmyparking.com. *Tirthayatris* could choose parking spots at eleven parking lots using a mobile application or website. Parking details were provided for two-wheelers, cars, buses, and tractors. The start-up tied up with a local company that managed parking sites and collected fees. Twist Mobile, an Indore-based start-up came up with a novel idea to reduce crowd pressure at the Mahakaleshvara Temple by providing virtual reality (VR) views of the temple's *bhasma arati*. The district administration loved this idea and gave the firm permission to shoot videos of the *arati* for six months. During the Kumbha, the firm set up 20 stalls with 5,000 Google

Cardboards (an affordable VR solution) and two Oculus Rift VR headsets. There were lines outside the stalls to have the VR views of *bhasma arati* at the cost of Rs 100 to Rs 250 per person. Medd, a healthcare start-up, provided preventive health checks for as low as Re. 1 at stalls, in addition to a mobile application for *tirthayatris* to book medical tests.

Another initiative at Ujjain in 2016 was the implementation of a telemedicine project following a directive from the Telemedicine Division of Ministry of Health and Family Welfare (MOHFW), Government of India. The project was a collaboration between Sanjay Gandhi Postgraduate Institute of Medical Sciences (SGPGI) in Lucknow, All India Institute of Medical Sciences (AIIMS) in Bhopal, and the Development Education Communication Unit (DECU) of Indian Space Research Organisation (ISRO) in Ahmedabad. A mobile telemedicine van was stationed at the Bhukhi Mata Sector in Datta Akhara Zone during the Mela. The van's satellite antenna was installed by ISRO-empanelled vendors. A team from ISRO helped in making the antenna operational and tested the connectivity with AIIMS Bhopal and SGPGI. The van had medical equipment for blood pressure and blood sugar measurement, ECG, dermatology, ophthalmology, ultrasound, and X-ray. Eight paramedical and technical personnel trained in using telemedicine software and Electronic Medical Records (EMRs) manned the van. Teleconsultation was provided by doctors in SGPGI and AIIMS from 9.30 am to 6 pm. Flyers in Hindi were distributed among *tirthayatris* to inform them about the telemedicine van. Over one month, 437 patients at the Mela were consulted by doctors in Lucknow and Bhopal using telemedicine. The van complemented the services of other medical facilities (including a 450-bed hospital) available at the Mela.

Kumbha Mela Experiment

A three-year project titled *The Kumbha Mela Experiment* was launched at the 2016 Ujjain Kumbha. Forty researchers (25 from India and 15 from the Netherlands, Russia, and Singapore) and 300 students (all from India) set up a research camp on 27,000 square feet of farmland in the Mela area. They collected data from GPS trackers, 1,000 wearable devices, mobile phones, CCTVs, drones, and cameras on balloons, poles, and vantage points. The goal of the project was to use big data analysis and Internet of Things (IoT) to understand crowd dynamics and predict crowd behaviour, including the probability of a stampede in the next 30 minutes. The study was funded by India's Department of Electronics and Information Technology (DeitY, now a full-fledged ministry) and Nederlandse Organisatie voor Wetenschappelijk Onderzoek (NWO), the national research council of the Netherlands. It had four universities as project coordinators and seven firms as industrial partners. The research team was led by Ashish Verma, a professor at the Indian Institute of Science (IISc). Prof. Verma and colleagues have published several papers on a range of topics including demographics and motivations, crowd dynamics, crowd safety and risk, and acceptable walking distance based on the data gathered during the experiment. In June 2018, the government think tank NITI Aayog counted the experiment among the best-use cases of Artificial Intelligence (AI) in the country.

Concluding Remarks

Tradition, commerce, and technology melt seamlessly at the modern Kumbha Mela. The Mela generates a revenue of several thousand crore rupees, providing a boost to the local economy and generating many jobs including thousands in the informal sector. The Mela necessitates major infrastructure upgrades in and around the host city. Several corporates have partnered with Mela administration to provide free water or sanitation services at the Mela. The use of technology is increasing with every iteration of the Mela. Technology solutions are being used to make the Mela more secure, make information available at *tirthayatris*' fingertips, reunite lost people with their families, and provide telemedicine services. The *saṅgacchadhvam* spirit of the traditionally modern Kumbha Mela makes tradition and modernity come together and enrich each other.

9. Diversity and Inclusivity

When UNESCO decided to include the Kumbha Mela in its Representative List of the Intangible Cultural Heritage of Humanity in December 2017, it noted the contribution of the Kumbha Mela to "cultural diversity and creativity, as well as tolerance and learning". India's nomination to UNESCO had stated that the Mela is "attended by millions of people irrespective of caste, creed or gender" and that it is "a culturally diverse festival".

These statements are not exaggerations. The Mela is as diverse and inclusive as any mass gathering event can get. Unlike the Hajj in Mecca which is closed to non-Muslims, the Kumbha Mela is open to people of all religions and even atheists. There are no checks, no declarations, and no constraints for anybody to attend the Kumbha Mela. The only unwritten rule is that participants are expected to experience the Kumbha, and not disrupt it as Christian missionaries tried to by distributing copies of the Bible at the 1855 Haridwar Kumbha (as documented by Robert Montgomery Martin).

Chapter 6 showed how some new-age religious movements which are very different from orthodox or traditional Hinduism have been welcomed at the Kumbha Mela for a long time. In this chapter, I show how the Mela welcomes people not only from Hindu communities which critics of Hinduism claim are marginalized within Hinduism, but also from communities outside Hinduism and foreign countries.

A Mela of All Hindus

It is often claimed that Hinduism discriminates on the basis of gender and caste against women and Dalits. One verse is quoted out of context from the *Manu Smriti* to claim that Hindu *dharmashastras* are against women, while the truth is that the same *Manu Smriti* boldly says that the gods rejoice where women are worshipped. One verse is similarly quoted from the *Purusha Sukta* to claim that caste hierarchy and discrimination is in-built in Vedic texts. The fact is that no hierarchy is implied in the said verse of the *Purusha Sukta* nor is any hierarchy interpreted in Sanskrit commentaries like those of Uvata or Mahidhara or in expositions of the verse by contemporary Hindu acharyas. Discrimination against women and Dalits in the Indian society is neither rooted in Hindu scriptures nor limited to Hindu communities. The Kumbha Mela, the greatest Hindu festival, is a testimony to the inclusivity of Hinduism.

Women

Crores of women participate in the Kumbha Mela. Around 40% of the people surveyed as part of *The Kumbha Mela Experiment* at the 2016 Ujjain Kumbha were females. At many religious gatherings in India, there are separate queues and areas for men and women. At the Kumbha Melas, however, men and women have mixed seamlessly without any inhibitions for centuries while bathing in the rivers. Captain Francis Raper observed at the 1808 Haridwar Kumbha, "the women even plunge in without hesitation, and both sexes intermix indiscriminately." I have experienced this at all the four Kumbha Melas I have been to. Neither are the women conscious while bathing in the river at the Mela, nor do the men at the Mela give any reason for them to become conscious. At Rama Kunda in Nashik, I even noticed some old women bathing in sarees without any upper garment in the presence of *tirthayatris* of both genders.

Women *sadhvis* and saints are also seen at the Kumbha Mela. Though far fewer in number compared to male sadhus and saints, they are showered with the same love and respect. One such example is Anandamayi Ma (1896–1982), who attended her first Kumbha Mela in 1927 when she was 31 years old. She participated in several Ardha Kumbha Melas and many Purna Kumbha Melas (at Haridwar in 1927, 1938, 1950, 1962, 1974; and at Prayaga in 1954, 1966, 1977). At the 1962 Haridwar Kumbha, she was honoured by the Niranjani Akhara which arranged an elephant for her to ride. At the 1966 Prayaga Kumbha, many leaders including Indira Gandhi paid her a visit. She was a part of the inaugural procession at the 1974 Haridwar Kumbha. At the 1977 Prayaga Kumbha, she arrived at the Kumbha Mela with the Mahanirvani Akhara and joined their procession on three main bathing days.

Surprising as it may sound to many, one comes across women Mahamandaleshvaras like Sadhvi Maitri Giri of the Juna Akhara at the Kumbha Melas. This is not a new trend. At the 1989 Prayaga Kumbha, Mark Tully was surprised to notice three women Mahamandaleshvaras, one of whom was declared a Mahamandaleshvara way back in 1974. The number of women getting honoured with the title has increased recently. Chetana Mata, a disciple of Pilot Baba, and Shraddha Mata were given the Mahamandaleshvara title at the 2007 Ardha Kumbha in Prayaga, while Prabha Mata was given the title at the Purna Kumbha in 2013. All three *sadhvis* belong to the Juna

Akhara. At the 2016 Ujjain Kumbha, the Agni Akhara bestowed the title of Mahamandaleshvara on a woman for the first time. The recipient was Kanakeshvari Devi, whose pandal ran the largest *anna kshetra* at the Ujjain Kumbha feeding 30,000 people every day. At the 2019 Ardha Kumbha in Prayaga, five women saints were made Mahamandaleshvaras by the Juna Akhara.

The Kumbha Melas have also been used as a platform to raise the issue of female infanticide. In 2013, a *Maa bachao, beti bachao* ("Save the mother, save the girl child") awareness drive was carried out from Hisar in Haryana to the Kumbha Mela in Prayaga. Led by Swami Ramabhagat and Sant Gopaladas, the drive was aimed at exhorting sadhus and saints to stress the importance of protecting cows (mothers) and daughters. The Shani Dham Trust also raised the issue of unbalanced sex ratio and female infanticide at the 2013 Prayaga Kumbha.

Scheduled castes and tribes

The Kumbha Mela is open to people of all castes. All public activities at the Mela—bathing in the river, visiting temples, listening to *katha* programmes, community meals (*bhandaras*), etc.—are open to everybody. Hindus of all castes mix with each other and eat and bathe side by side. Most *shiviras* are also open for everybody to come inside and take a look. The inclusive nature of Hinduism is seen in practice at the Mela.

Many Dalit *tirthayatris* are part of the Kumbha Mela. And if one observes carefully, tribals are also seen at the Kumbha Mela. Mark Tully reported the presence of barefoot girls from tribes of central India who wore thick silver anklets at the 1989 Prayaga Kumbha. The Saregama Shakti documentary on the

2010 Haridwar Kumbha showed several tribal women from Rajasthan, wearing numerous white plastic bangles in their upper and lower arms.

The Kumbha Mela has also been used as a platform to reach out to *tirthayatris* and sadhus from the Dalit communities. At the 2013 Prayaga Kumbha, around 100 Dalit women who were formerly manual scavengers bathed alongside conch-blowing Brahmin priests at the Sangama. The Dalit women stayed at the camps of sadhus and dined with Swami Narendra Giri, head of ABAP. Similarly, around 200 Dalit women from Rajasthan who were formerly scavengers bathed with Brahmin priests chanting Sanskrit verses and mantras in the Shipra at the 2016 Ujjain Kumbha. Pandit Umashankar Tiwari, one of the priests present, hoped that this programme would help promote equality in society. Both these programmes were organized by Bindeshwar Pathak of the Sulabh Shauchalaya movement. At the 2015 Nashik Kumbha, BJP President Amit Shah attended a joint bathing programme called the *Samajika Samarasata Snana* ("bath for social equality") with sadhus from both Dalit and non-Dalit communities. Another *Samarasata Snana* was held at the 2016 Ujjain Kumbha where many Dalits and tribals were invited. Although some political analysts saw this as an attempt by the ruling BJP to woo Dalits and tribals, it found many supporters also. Tribal dance artiste Bharat Baria called it a big achievement and said, "Politics is above all this. We should look at the message of unity that comes across from this." In 2018, the ABAP announced that Dalits would also be ordained as Naga sadhus during the 2019 Ardha Kumbha at Prayaga. In the 2019 Mela, the Juna Akhara ordained Kanhaiya Prabhu Nand Giri, a Dalit sadhu, as a Mahamandaleshvara.

At the upcoming 2025 Kumbha in Prayaga, 71 people from deprived classes (scheduled castes and scheduled tribes) will be conferred the title of Mahamandaleshvara by the Juna Akhara. Many others will be made Mahantas and Mandaleshvaras.

Nepalis

For all practical purposes, Nepalis are not foreigners to India. No passport or visa is required for Nepalese citizens entering India from Nepal, just an identity document is enough (for children below ten years, even that is not needed). For many generations, Hindu *tirthayatris* from Nepal have been visiting the Kumbha Mela. Many are immediately identifiable from their traditional caps (*Dhaka topis*), as Mark Tully noted during the 1989 Prayaga Kumbha. At the 2010 Haridwar Kumbha, a middle-aged Nepali man who was travelling with his parents told Saregama Shakti that he was attending his fourth Kumbha at Haridwar. The Nepali *tirthayatris* comfortably speak Hindi and mingle freely with the crowds at the Kumbha Mela.

Many Nepalis and Indians of Nepali origin play a significant role in activities at the Kumbha Melas. Nepal has a thriving Shukla Yajur Veda tradition which has dwindled in many parts of northern India. Vedic scholars from Nepal like Acharya Chandradatta Suvedi, who I have known for many years, have long been associated with religious organizations in India and perform *havana*s as priests during the Kumbha Mela. The prolific author and Patanjali Group CEO Acharya Balkrishna (also born to a Suvedi family) is an Indian citizen of Nepali descent who plays an important role in Patanjali Yogpeeth's large-scale participation in Kumbha Melas.

Transgenders

On 15 April 2014, the Supreme Court of India passed a landmark judgement in the National Legal Services Authority versus Union of India case. The judgement recognized the transgenders as a "third gender" and issued multiple directives to the Centre and State Governments including providing separate public toilets and other facilities and making them feel that they are part and parcel of the social life in India.

On Dussehra in 2015, a new *akhara* called the Kinnara Akhara was set up by transgenders in Ujjain as a result of efforts by Ajay Das and Laxmi Narayan Tripathi. The word *kinnara* (किन्नर), which refers to a class of horse-faced deities in Sanskrit, is used in Hindi for transgender people. The Kinnara Akhara participated just like any other organization in the 2016 Ujjain Kumbha. The Mela administration made special arrangements for transgenders at Ujjain. Special toilets called *Kinnara Shauchalaya*s were made available for transgenders. Ajay Das, patron of the *akhara*, told the media at Ujjain that while a majority of transgenders are Hindus when they join the community, their dominant religion is Islam. He added that the participation of transgenders in the Kumbha was like a homecoming for them because they embraced Hinduism by wearing saffron robes. The *akhara*'s stage at the Ujjain Kumbha had the backdrop of Ardhanarishvara, the half-female and half-male form of Shiva. The *akhara* took part in the 2019 Prayaga Ardha Kumbha also. While the ABAP did not grant recognition to the Kinnara Akhara, it agreed to initiate transgenders as *samnyasi*s in August 2018. The ABAP said that transgenders would be free to choose from any of the thirteen *akhara*s which were its members.

Non-Hindus at Kumbha Mela

For the upcoming 2025 Kumbha at Prayaga, the ABAP proposed that "non-Sanatani" people, with the exception of Sikhs, Jains and Buddhists, be disallowed from entering or setting stalls at the Kumbha Mela. It is unlikely that the authorities will enforce any such rule. Historically, non-Hindus, including followers of Abrahamic faiths, have been free to participate in Kumbha Melas.

Sikhs

Many Sikhs participate in Hindu festivals and visit Hindu temples, freely blending with the Hindu crowds. I have seen with my own eyes a Sikh family praying with a pandit at the Kashi Vishwanath temple in Varanasi. The Kumbha Mela attracts a small number of Sikh sadhus and *tirthayatris*. The Nirmala Akhara (see chapter 4) of Sikh sadhus is one of the thirteen traditional *akharas* at the Kumbha Mela. At the 2013 Prayaga Kumbha, several Sikh men and women attended the daily evening *arati* of the *Guru Grantha Sahib* at the Nirmala Akhara *shivira*. At the same Mela, Mark Stratton wrote about meeting a Californian Sikh named Ravinder Singh who had come to visit his guru Jagtar Muni (Shri Mahanta, Naya Udasina Akhara). A documentary on the 2016 Ujjain Kumbha by Harshit Jain showed a young Sikh boy, identified by his black patka, bathing and praying in the Shipra just like Hindus.

In recent years, Sikh individuals and organizations have contributed indirectly to the Kumbha Melas. In 2013, the Shiromani Gurudwara Prabandhak Committee (SGPC) decided to participate in the Prayaga Kumbha Mela on the invitation of the Rashtriya Swayamsevak Sangh (RSS). Despite opposition by some radical Sikh organizations like Dal Khalsa, the SGPC went ahead. It set up a photo exhibition, arranged a *langar* service (community kitchen), and displayed books on Sikhism published in Hindi. Avtar Singh Makkar, the then SGPC chief, stated that there was evidence of Guru Nanak participating in the Haridwar Kumbha Mela and that the Gurudwara Gyan Godri Sahib (which stands at Har Ki Pauri in Haridwar) was a testimony to this. At the 2016 Ujjain Kumbha, a group of Sikhs travelled from Punjab and set up an *anna kshetra* to provide free food to *tirthayatris*. The Sikhs were proud that this was their and Punjab's contribution to the Mela.

Jains

A unique confluence of Hinduism and Jainism was seen at the 2016 Ujjain Kumbha, when a Jain *sadhvi* was made a Mahamandaleshvara of the Juna Akhara on 12 May in the presence of Hindu and Jain sadhus. Swami Avadheshananda Giri whispered a mantra in the ears of Sadhvi Chandanaprabha, who wore ochre clothes and was given ochre robes as per the tradition of Juna Akhara in the ceremony. The *sadhvi* took on the new name Chandanaprabhananda Giri. The *sadhvi* was initiated by the legendary Jain sadhu Acharya Tulasi (1914–97) in 1981 and now considers Swami Hari Giri of the Juna Akhara as her guru. She said she would follow the traditions of both Jainism and Hinduism and act as a bridge between the two religions. During the Mela, her *shivira* attracted many Jains from Ujjain and outside, organized a programme where 1008 Jain couples worshipped the Jain goddess Padmavati (protector of Parshvanatha), and ran an *anna kshetra* which served free food without onion and garlic till sunset every day.

Bathing in rivers, believing them to be sacred, is criticized in Jain traditions as *loka-mudhata* ("folly of the world"). Bathing in rivers and considering them sacred is an integral part of Hindu traditions and is the *raison d'être* of the Kumbha Mela. The *saṅgacchadhvam* spirit of the Kumbha Mela brought Hindu and Jain saints and masses together at Ujjain despite such antipodal differences.

Muslims

Although extremely rare, there are examples of Muslims taking part in the Kumbha Mela. Shameem Ahmed, originally from Azamgarh, is a railway shunting master settled in Aligarh. Ahmed has been bathing in the Ganga since 1983. He has taken part in the 2001 and 2013 Purna Kumbha Melas and the 2007 Ardha Kumbha Mela at Prayaga. Just like a traditional Hindu, Ahmed has preserved *gangajala* ("water of Ganga") for many years. Another example is Anwar Mohammed, who played the *shehnai* (a double-reeded wind instrument popular in northern India) for many years as part of the bathing procession of the Niranjani Akhara. In 2013, he was initiated as a sadhu in the Niranjani Akhara. There may be others like Ahmed and Mohammed, Muslims by religion and Hindu by culture, who have participated in the Kumbha Mela. Hindus are barred from entering Mecca, but Muslims like Ahmed and Mohammed are not prevented from taking part in the Kumbha Mela.

Maulana Kalbe Sadiq (1939–2020), a Shia Muslim leader from Lucknow, announced in 2009 that he would take a dip at the Haridwar Kumbha in 2010 to cement the bond between

Hindus and Muslims. He attended a gathering of religious leaders at the 2016 Ujjain Kumbha at the invitation of Chidananda Muni.

At times, Muslims have shown their support to the Kumbha Melas. In 2010, Haridwar's Muslims—who welcome annual Kanwar pilgrims by offering them fruits and juice—put up Hindi banners to welcome sadhus and saints to the Haridwar Kumbha. During the 2013 Prayaga Kumbha, Azam Khan was the head of the Kumbha Mela management committee. The Minority Affairs department in the central and state governments in India is usually held by a person from the minority community. In contrast, here was an example of a person from the minority (Muslim) community heading the management of the biggest fair of the majority community (Hindus). In July 2018, Muslims of Prayagraj voluntarily demolished parts of several mosques to make way for widening of the city's roads for the 2019 Ardha Kumbha. This move was praised by officials of the Prayagraj Development Authority.

Christians

While a lot of foreigners at the Kumbha Mela are associated with a Hindu organization and follow some Hindu practices, many others are Christians. They are still welcomed openly at the Mela, sometimes even by traditional acharyas, without any requirement to convert to Hinduism. M. Darrol Bryant, Distinguished Professor Emeritus of Religious Studies at the Renison College (University of Waterloo) and a practising Christian, has both experienced the Kumbha Mela (as a guest of the Goswami family of the Shri Radha Raman Mandir) and written about it. His following words, written in 2002, are a glowing tribute to the inclusive nature of the Kumbha Mela and the Hindus at the Mela:

> Perhaps in no other event in the Hindu world is the faith of Hindus so remarkably unveiled as in the Kumbha Mela. My task as a Christian is to try to understand that faith. I was welcomed to their Festival, not only by the Goswami family but by everyone I met there. Through my participation in the Kumbha Mela, I was able to draw closer to the Hindu pilgrims whose inner world of belief and gesture was not mine. I have come away deeply grateful for their openness to my presence and impressed by the depth of their devotion.

Buddhists

While Buddhists do not participate in the Kumbha Mela, there are some exceptions like Shanthum Seth, a Buddhist writer and an ordained *dharmacharya* in the Zen lineage of the Vietnamese monk Thích Nhất Hạnh. Seth camped for a full month at the 2013 Prayaga Kumbha. As per Seth, he was on this pilgrimage since "Buddha advises to go on pilgrimage."

The fourteenth Dalai Lama, Tenzin Gyatso, has been a frequent visitor at the Kumbha Melas at the invitation of Hindu religious leaders. It is the mutual respect for each other's beliefs and traditions that makes this happen. In 2001, the Dalai Lama visited the Prayaga Kumbha. He performed the *arati* of Ganga with several Hindu religious leaders including Chidananda Muni and spoke about Hinduism and Buddhism, describing them as twin sisters. In 2013 also, he was scheduled to visit the Prayaga Kumbha but his visit was cancelled at the last moment due to security reasons. He has been a visitor at other Kumbha Melas too. In 2010, he attended a series of programmes at the Haridwar Kumbha and launched the book "Encyclopaedia of Hinduism". In addition, he participated in a *shastrartha* on Sankhya philosophy with Swami Sharanananda. During the 2015 Nashik-Tryambakeshwar Kumbha, he took a symbolic dip in Kushavarta Kunda by sprinkling water on his head. He was scheduled to visit the 2016 Ujjain Kumbha, but cancelled his visit at the last moment due to health reasons. Dölma Gyari, the then Home Kalon of the Central Tibetan Administration, did attend the fair at Ujjain and participated in the *Rashtra-raksha Mahayajna* held for world peace and strength, prosperity, and security of India.

Foreigners

Foreigners have been attracted to the Kumbha Mela for a long time. In recent times, an increasing number of foreigners have attended the Mela multiple times and have loved the experience just like Indians. Notable among such foreigners are Ramdas Lamb, Maria Wirth, Yvette Rosser, and Stephen Knapp. While many such foreigners are practising Hindus, many others are not. The 2010 Haridwar Kumbha saw thousands of foreigners camp in Haridwar. A large number of solo travellers came from countries like Argentina, China, France, Russia, Spain, Switzerland, and the United Kingdom. Lakhs of foreigners were present at the 2013 Prayaga Kumbha. Many of them were associated with an organization like the Paramartha Niketana Ashram, the TM movement, or ISKCON;

many others came in small groups; many travelled as individual participants; and some participated in the Mela even as sadhus. Many African followers of ISKCON participated in the 2016 Ujjain Kumbha and sang and danced in groups.

In an episode of *Sacred Journeys with Bruce Feiler*, author and adventurer Bruce Feiler profiled several groups of people who travelled from the United States to participate in the 2013 Prayaga Kumbha. The diversity in these groups was truly remarkable. They included a middle-aged Hindu businessman from California who was born in India, his white American wife who was born a Catholic but converted to Hinduism, a Californian woman of East-European origin who was formerly a nurse and health executive, yoga instructors from Florida including a young Sikh man, a real-estate developer of Iranian origin from Colorado, a woman ecologist from Colorado, and a 23-year-old Jewish male who was studying medicine in New York. Some of these *tirthayatris* prepared for the experience of a bath in cold water at the Kumbha by taking an early-morning bath in the Ganga at Varanasi before they reached Prayaga.

Foreigners freely mingling with Indian *tirthayatris* and nonchalantly moving around in the large crowds at Kumbha Melas is a common sight. The 2013 Prayaga Kumbha started just one month after the horrific Nirbhaya gangrape that happened in Delhi on 16 December 2012. Shortly after the gangrape, several foreign governments had cautioned travellers visiting India and leading foreign newspapers had published articles on why India was not safe for solo women travellers. Despite this, thousands of foreign women travellers were at the Prayaga Kumbha Mela. A woman from Brazil travelled alone and stayed for a full month in Prayaga, as

Shambhu Mishra told Bruce Feiler. In the two days I spent at Prayaga Kumbha, I saw quite a few foreigners, including solo women. If their nonchalance was anything to go by, the Kumbha Mela was indeed safe for solo women travellers.

Finally, there are foreigner sadhus too at the Kumbha Mela. Their acceptance among sadhus has grown in recent times. Three sadhus—Baba Rama Puri (also known as Beverly Hills Baba), Mangalananda Puri, and Vasudeva Puri—became the first foreigners to be ordained as Shri Mahanta of the Juna Akhara at the 2010 Haridwar Kumbha. In 2013, Rama Puri told Diego Buñuel of the National Geographic that it took him 20 years to figure out what was happening in the world of sadhus and another five years to be accepted. Yogmata Keiko Aikawa, a Japanese woman said to have realized *samadhi*, was another major attraction at the 2013 Prayaga Kumbha.

Journalists and Researchers

The inclusivity of the Kumbha Mela extends to journalists and researchers also. The experience of the French-Spanish adventurer journalist Diego Buñuel at the 2013 Prayaga Kumbha is a great example. As he admitted later, Buñuel came to the Kumbha Mela with several prejudices. However, he left the Mela with surreal feelings after staying with Naga sadhus for 24 days and learning their ways. Buñuel's interpreter Saurabh introduced him to Rajarajeshvara Giri, his guru of 24 days, as *"Yeh Diego Ji hain"* ("This is the respectable Diego"). Rajarajeshvara Giri immediately opened up and asked in English, "Hello Diego, how are you?" Following the pleasantries, Buñuel touched the feet of Rajarajeshvara Giri.

Rajarajeshvara Giri freely spoke with Buñuel about the life of Naga sadhus and also invited him to be a part of the main bathing procession on *Mauni Amavasya*. During his bath, Buñuel noticed a sadhu who he had met with on his first day at the Mela, and both of them instantly recognized each other. When he left the Kumbha Mela, Buñuel had feelings similar to those that he felt when he watched films by his grandfather, Luis Buñuel.

There were several research teams at the 2013 Prayaga Kumbha. A five-member team representing the Bihar State Disaster Management Authority (BSDMA) camped at the Mela with the aim to study its operational planning and outline good practices and gaps to derive recommendations for other mass gathering events in India. Their case study is freely available on the BSDMA website. A seven-member research team from Tata Institute of Social Sciences (TISS) and Doctors For You (DFY) was given permission for conducting their field work by the Mela administration during the 2013 Prayaga Kumbha. Their report was published in the journal *PLOS Currents Disasters* and is freely accessible. A multi-disciplinary research team from Harvard University was at the same Kumbha to study the Mela from urban planning, business, religious studies, public health, and governance perspectives. The research led to the case studies "Kumbh Mela: India's Pop-up Mega-City" and "Kumbh Mela: Mapping the Ephemeral Mega City". Ironically, at Rs 650 and Rs 2000 respectively, both these publications on the biggest festival of humanity are inhumanely priced, in sharp contrast to the two studies mentioned earlier. Perhaps the Mela administrators should enforce that any such research done on the Kumbha Mela be made available freely or at a reasonable cost. *The Kumbha Mela Experiment* at the 2016 Ujjain Kumbha involved forty researchers from four countries, three hundred students from India, and many local volunteers. The Mela administration provided 27,000 square feet of space for setting up the research camp for the project.

Holi at the Kumbha

Holi, the egalitarian ancient Hindu festival of colours, falls in the end of February or the first half of March on the full moon day of the *Phalguna* lunar month. The Haridwar Kumbha is the only Kumbha during which Holi falls—the Prayaga Kumbha ends on *Maha Shivaratri*, which falls around a fortnight before Holi, and the Ujjain and Nashik-Tryambakeshwar Kumbhas start much after Holi. While Haridwar is not as famous for Holi as places like Mathura, Ayodhya, or Varanasi, Holi during the Haridwar Kumbha Mela is celebrated with great fervour. The presence of many sadhus and *tirthayatris* from various states added to the festive spirit of Holi at the 2010 Haridwar Kumbha. Sadhus and saints visited each other's *shivira*s and smeared each other with *abir* and *gulal*. In addition to fellow sadhus and their gurus, sadhus of the Juna Akhara played Holi with the *murti*s of Dattatreya, Shiva, and Ganesha. This was a day when Shaiva Naga sadhus were seen covered in red powder rather than grey ash.

Experience, but No Disruption

The Kumbha Mela is open to one and all for experiencing, but disruption of the Mela is not welcome. Of late, the Akhila Bharatiya Akhara Parishad (ABAP) has been taking steps to prevent controversial and/or convicted religious or spiritual personalities from attending the Kumbha. In September 2017, ABAP declared fourteen such people as "fake". ABAP President Narendra Giri said that these people would not be allowed to get government facilities in the Ardha Kumbha and Purna Kumbha Melas. The list included some popular names like Asaram Bapu, Radhe Maa, Sacchidananda Giri, Gurmeet Ram Rahim Singh, Om Baba, Nirmal Baba, Bhimananda Maharaja, Aseemananda, Narayan Sai, and Rampal. More such names were released by the ABAP on 29 December 2017, 16 March 2018, and 2 April 2018.

The Juna Akhara banned the entry of foreigners at their *shivira* in the 2013 Prayaga Kumbha, noticing that foreigners were bringing in liquor and drugs to lure sadhus. Three sadhus were also expelled for this reason. In addition, sadhus of the *akhara* were also concerned about some sadhus luring Western women into marriages. Other *akharas* continued to entertain foreigners. Though it welcomed the decision of the Juna Akhara, the Nirvani Akhara said that foreigners would be free to come to its *shivira* and explore their curiosities.

Concluding Remarks

The Kumbha Mela is a religious and spiritual festival where faith is paramount. As Vibhav Bhushan Uphadhyaya told Mark Tully in 1989, "The Kumbh Mela is one of the rituals of *dharma*. You come here because you have faith in *dharma* and its rituals, not because you hope to get faith. Without faith you cannot really expect to understand the Mela." I believe that all visitors, whether Indians or foreigners, should strive to respect the faith of the sadhus, the *kalpavasis*, and *tirthayatris* at the Mela. As long as they do so, the *saṅgacchadhvam* spirit of the Kumbha Mela welcomes them with open arms, irrespective of their gender, caste, religion, nationality, or ideology. This is what makes the Kumbha Mela an unbelievably diverse and inclusive celebration.

10. The Immortal Mela

It is believed that the Kumbha Mela is held at the places where the divine nectar of immortality fell on the earth. In a sense, the Mela itself is an immortal festival. The tradition of the *Magha-snana* has been dated to the Neolithic times by D. K. Roy and while its form and designation may have changed over time, there is no doubt that the tradition of the Kumbha Mela has been around for millennia. The Mela tradition has survived Islamic invasions of India, Muslim rule, British rule, internecine conflicts, two World Wars, and the global COVID-19 pandemic. The Mela tradition has survived thousands of deaths due to cholera epidemics, stampedes, and natural calamities. The Mela has seen heart-rending moments like the immersion of Lal Bahadur Shastri's ashes at the 1966 Kumbha Mela. The Mela tradition continued during the 1975–77 Emergency, the darkest period of Indian democracy. The Mela tradition survived rumours in 1989 that lakhs would be killed in a stampede. Despite all these, life at the Kumbha Mela has never stopped. The Kumbha Mela has been called "the greatest show on earth", and it is also the greatest example of the principle that come what may, "the show must go on."

Timur's Attack

After his conquest of Delhi, the Turco-Mongol invader Timur sacked the city of Haridwar and massacred many pilgrims in early 1399. Several authors have suggested that this possibly happened at a Kumbha Mela. This is confirmed by astronomical evidence which shows that 1399 was the year of the Ardha Kumbha at Haridwar. As per Swiss Ephemeris and the Lahiri Ayanamsha value of 15°23′ for 1392, Jupiter entered Aquarius (as per *nirayana* reckoning) in December 1392. This implies that the Kumbha Mela was held in 1393 at Haridwar. The 7-in-83 thumb rule of chapter 2 also gives 1393 as the year of Kumbha Mela at Haridwar (Haridwar had a Kumbha Mela in 1974 and $1974 - 7 \times 83 = 1393$). With the Kumbha in 1393, 1399 would be the year of the Ardha Kumbha and it is likely that the massacre of pilgrims at Haridwar happened at the Ardha Kumbha Mela.

Muslim and British Rule

The Muslim rule of northern India started with the Delhi Sultanate in the beginning of the thirteenth century and lasted till the Maratha Empire replaced the Mughals in the middle of the eighteenth century. The traditions of the Magha Mela and the Kumbha Mela survived though many Hindu temples, seats of learning, and traditions perished. The *akharas* of sadhus armed themselves and kept their Mela tradition alive. The Mughal emperor Akbar built a large fort on the banks of the Yamuna near the Mela area. The fort enclosed several sacred Hindu sites near the Sangama—the Patalpuri temple, the Sarasvati Kupa, and the Akshaya Vata—and isolated them from the site of the Mela. Prayaga, the name of the holiest Hindu site, was changed to Ilahabas by Akbar and Ilahabad later by Shah Jahan. These appropriative changes would have certainly disheartened lakhs of Hindu sadhus and *tirthayatris*, but they preserved the Mela tradition.

Under the rule of the East India Company, *tirthayatris* to Prayaga were heavily taxed for nearly thirty years in the early nineteenth century. The number of *tirthayatris* at the Magha and the Kumbha Melas reduced, but the Mela tradition lived on. The Mela later grew in scale under the British Raj with improvement in road and rail infrastructure and medical, health, and sanitation facilities in the host cities.

During the World Wars

The 1915 Haridwar Kumbha was held in the year of the First World War, in which the British Indian Army was involved right from 1914. The British authorities, who were stretched, were helped by several Indian volunteer organizations in the organization of the Kumbha. Gopal Krishna Gokhale's Servants of India Society (SIS) sent a large group of volunteers, which was joined by the Phoenix Party of Mahatma Gandhi. Around 17 lakh people attended the 1915 Haridwar Kumbha.

The 1942 Prayaga Kumbha was held during the Second World War. The British government in India feared that Japan may bomb Akbar's Fort, which was also a military installation, resulting in many casualties. The government made no preparations or expenses for the Mela (as funds were needed for the war), banned the sale of rail tickets to Prayagraj, and also issued an advisory against mass gatherings for pilgrims. The attendance at the Mela was heavily reduced, but the Mela was still held and lakhs of sadhus and *tirthayatris* gathered to carry forward the tradition.

An anecdote about the 1942 Prayaga Kumbha has been published by many Indian newspapers. When Lord Linlithgow (the then Viceroy of India) and Pandit Madan Mohan Malaviya saw the lakhs of people at the 1942 Mela, Linlithgow wondered how much money was spent on publicity to gather so many people. "Two paise," Pandit Malaviya replied. When a shocked Linlithgow asked Malaviya how it was possible, Malaviya took out a *panchanga* and told him that it cost two paise to print a *panchanga*, from which common Hindus would know when the Mela would be held and nobody is sent any invitations. I do not know if such a conversation really happened between Linlithgow and Malaviya, but that no invitations are sent to the lakhs of sadhus, *kalpavasis*, and *tirthayatris* coming to the Mela is an undeniable fact.

Cholera at Kumbha Mela

Several iterations of the Kumbha Mela have been hit by cholera epidemics. As per the account of John Macpherson, 20,000 *tirthayatris* died at the 1783 Haridwar Kumbha, which drew an estimated 20 lakh visitors. Between 1879 to 1948, the number of deaths due to cholera in United Provinces were very high in the years when the 24 Ardha and Purna Kumbha Melas at Haridwar and Prayaga were held. While not many died during the Mela (in the years of the Haridwar Kumbha, most deaths occurred between April and December after the Mela), but the Mela was where cholera infection spread. For the first time, cholera inoculation was made compulsory in the 1945 Ardha Kumbha at Haridwar. People who were not inoculated were prevented from entering within a 16 km radius of the Mela.

There were no cholera cases reported at the Mela that year. This led to compulsory cholera inoculation at the Kumbha Mela during much of the 1950s, 1960s, and 1970s. The compulsory inoculation is now no longer required. This is probably because better medical care and sanitation facilities are now available at the Kumbha Mela.

Tribute to a Beloved Prime Minister

On 25 January 1965, the moon of gloom eclipsed the sun of joy at the Prayaga Kumbha Mela. The previous day, 24 January, was *Mauni Amavasya*, the most sacred day for bathing at the Prayaga Kumbha. It was also the day when Indira Gandhi was sworn in as the new Prime Minister of India in New Delhi. On 25 January, the Prime Minister arrived in a special train from Delhi at the Kumbha Mela to immerse the ashes of India's beloved former Prime Minister Lal Bahadur Shastri who had passed away in Tashkent two weeks earlier (on 11 January). The government had relaxed the inoculation requirement for that day to enable more people to attend the immersion ceremony.

End of a Dark Night

The Emergency imposed by Prime Minister Indira Gandhi from 1975 to 1977 is widely considered as the darkest period of Indian democracy. Elections to the Lok Sabha were suspended, rights of people were restricted, leaders of opposition parties were imprisoned, and criticism from the press was censored. The 1977 Prayaga Kumbha was held in such a dark period. However, the sun of hope rose on the sacred day of *Mauni*

Amavasya. As lakhs of faithful Hindus bathed in the Sangama in Prayaga on 18 January 1977, Lok Sabha elections were announced on radio. The Kumbha Nagari was soon in a festive mood following the announcement. The dark night had ended on the most sacred day of the Kumbha Mela, the festival where life triumphs over death, hope over despair, optimism over pessimism, and light over darkness.

Natural Calamities

Many Kumbha Melas have been hit in the past by natural calamities. However, no calamity has been strong enough to defeat the spirit of the sadhus or the *tirthayatris*. Rains played havoc during the 2013 Prayaga Kumbha on 16 February, with a record 60 mm rainfall in 24 hours. All 18 gates of the Kumbha Nagari collapsed along with many electric poles, resulting in a complete blackout in some sectors. Thirty-five people were injured and admitted to hospitals in the Kumbha Nagari and in Prayagraj city. Around 20,000 tents were submerged knee-deep in water. The Mela administration vacated 26 schools for people to shift. Many police and PAC personnel also shifted to the schools, but a large number of *kalpavasis* stayed back. Ramawati Devi from Madhya Pradesh told India Today that the *kalpavasis* were there because of the Sangama and they did not even mind dying at the Sangama.

At the 2016 Ujjain Kumbha, a heavy rainstorm hit the Mela on the afternoon of 5 May, four days after I had been to the Mela. Seven people died and around one hundred were injured as many pandals and gates collapsed. Rescue operations were difficult due to the slush, but most of the pilgrims stayed back and started taking dips again in the night. Normalcy was restored by the next day. Chief Minister Shivraj Singh Chouhan reached Ujjain next morning at 4 am and spent five hours overseeing relief work. Around one third of the tents at the Mela were partly or fully blown away by the wind. It took one week to set them up again, but the Mela continued as usual.

Stampedes

One of the biggest tragedies at the Kumbha Mela in pre-independent India occurred in the 1820 Haridwar Kumbha, when a stampede killed more than 400 people. Several stampedes have occurred at the Haridwar Kumbha in independent India, killing 20 people in 1950, 50 in 1986, and five in 2010. On 27 August 2003, 39 people were killed in stampede at the Nashik Kumbha.

During the 1954 Prayaga Kumbha, there was a stampede which killed many hundreds and injured thousands of pilgrims. As a result, elephants were banned in the following Kumbha Melas till 1989. They were back, however, in the 2001 and 2013 melas. On *Mauni Amavasya* (10 February) of the 2013 Prayaga Kumbha, 38 people were killed in a stampede at the Prayagraj railway station (outside the Kumbha Nagari). The stampede was triggered when a foot-over-bridge collapsed on a platform.

During the 1989 Prayaga Kumbha, there were widespread rumours that the BBC had reported that two lakh people will be killed in a stampede at the Mela. Mark Tully wrote about how he heard it from multiple people, from people as diverse as the then mayor of Prayagraj and the boatmen at Prayaga.

Despite the rumours, lakhs turned out on the *Mauni Amavasya* day, much to the relief of the Mela administration.

The COVID-19 Pandemic

The 2021 Kumbha Mela at Haridwar was held during the COVID-19 pandemic. Many feared that the Mela would become a super-spreader event. As mentioned in chapter 2, the Haridwar Kumbha Mela is usually held from January to April. For example, the 2010 Mela was held from 14 January to 28 April. In 2021, in light of the pandemic, the Mela duration was shortened to one month, from 1 April to 30 April. A standard operating procedure (SOP) was released and widely distributed. A negative RT-PCR test report within 72 hours of entry into the Mela area was mandatory for all visitors.

Unfortunately, a deadly second wave of COVID-19 infections broke out in India in early April. On 9 April, the active case count in India exceeded 10 lakh. Despite all precautions, thousands of *tirthayatris* and dozens of sadhus tested positive for COVID-19 in the Haridwar Mela. On 14 April, 10–13 lakh people (estimates vary) bathed in the Ganga at Haridwar. On 15 April, Mahamandaleshvara Kapil Dev Das of the Nirvani Akhara died of COVID-19 complications in the Mela area. Following this, two *akharas* announced their exit from the Mela. On 17 April, Prime Minister Narendra Modi spoke with Avadheshananda Giri of the Juna Akhara and appealed for an end to the Mela, stating that it should only be symbolic for the rest of the days. Avadheshananda Giri agreed and requested people not to come in large numbers to Haridwar and follow all rules. The appeals and the second wave of the pandemic had an impact: only 25,000 people turned up for the third shahi *snana* on 27 April. In all, around 91 lakh people participated in the 2021 Kumbha at Haridwar. The number of visitors was less than one-fifth of the number of visitors at the 2010 Haridwar Kumbha.

Concluding Remarks

The Kumbha Mela is a celebration of life. And like life, it has not always been blissful and peaceful at the Mela. There have been invasions, disease outbreaks, natural calamities, and stampedes due to which thousands have died at the Mela. The Mela has seen reduced crowds due to high taxes and wars. The Mela has seen India's prosperity fall and start to rise again. Despite all these ups and downs, the Mela has not stopped, like life does not stop. Whatever the situation, our *jijivisha* (जिजीविषा, "desire to live") finds a way, and so does the Kumbha Mela.

11. Personal Experiences

How does one describe a blissful experience in words? Is it even possible? In Tulasidasa's *Ramacharitamanasa*, one of Sita's confidantes who has just seen Rama and Lakshmana expresses her helplessness while describing the reason for her excessive joy. She says "How shall I describe them? The speech is without vision and the eyes are without the ability to speak." These inabilities hold completely true when it comes to describing the Kumbha Mela experience. If a faculty could both perceive and express, an accurate description of the experience could be possible. None of the organs of perception (*jnanendriya*s)—the eyes that saw the spectacular scenes at the Kumbha, the ears that heard the continuum of human voices and music at the Kumbha, the nose that smelt the fragrance of incense-sticks and camphor at the Kumbha, the skin that touched the soothing waters of the Sangama at the Kumbha, and the tongue which tasted the *sattvika* food served at the Kumbha—is able to express the experience in words. To experience the Kumbha Mela, one has to visit the Mela where all these experiences combine together to momentarily take the believer into a different blissful world altogether. Despite the limitations, I make an attempt to describe my experiences at four Kumbha Melas: Prayaga Kumbha (2013), Nashik-Tryambakeshwar Kumbha (2015), Ujjain Kumbha (2016), and Prayaga Ardha Kumbha (2019). Most of this chapter is about my experiences at the 2013 Kumbha and the 2019 Ardha

Kumbha.

Prayaga: 2013

During the Kumbha Mela at Prayaga in 2013, I was working in Hong Kong and was on a visit to my firm's Mumbai office from 14 to 18 January. I decided to visit the Mela for a couple of days before flying back to Hong Kong. Many of my Indian friends and almost all of my Indian colleagues were surprised to know that I was visiting the Kumbha. I do not blame them, but the stereotypes prevalent about the Kumbha Mela among urban Indians and the scorn with which the English media in India has treated the Kumbha Mela over the years (as Mark Tully has rightly pointed out). The first question they asked was, "What for?" My answer was a crisp one, "To experience firsthand the greatest festival on the earth." Their other questions displayed a complete lack of information about the Kumbha. "Is the place clean?" "What about sanitation?" "What if there is a stampede?" "Is it not dangerous?" My answers helped allay some of the stereotypes they had held for years.

All the major hotels were booked in Prayagraj, Swiss tents were too expensive, and I was not sure if I could survive the biting cold of Prayaga in a *shivira*. I was fortunate to find accommodation online at Kanchan Villa, a colonial-era bungalow at Lukerganj which is now partly converted to a hotel. Little did I know that I would find the Mela so refreshing that I would spend hardly any time apart from six or seven hours during the nights at the villa. On the evening of 18 January, I flew from Mumbai to Lucknow. I spent the night at my ancestral home in Lucknow and set out for Prayagraj early morning on the next day. At the wheel was Ajay Varma, a friend and the owner of a taxi service business in Lucknow.

After checking in at Kanchan Villa, Ajay and I shortly set out for the Kumbha Nagari from Lukerganj. Along the way we crossed the Rupa Gaudiya Matha, the Alopi Devi Mandir, and the Naga Vasuki Mandir. As we were entering the sandy Kumbha Nagari, we saw a robed sadhu asking us for a lift. As a rule, I never stop to give lift to strangers anywhere. But there was something in the air that day. Without a moment's thought, Ajay immediately stopped the car and I opened the door for the sadhu. We asked him where he had to go. He said he had to be dropped at one of the *shivira*s. None of us knew where that was with the countless *shivira*s visible. But we thought we will find out. Shortly, the sadhu located the banner of his *shivira* and asked us to stop. We stopped, he got down. We both bowed down to him, he blessed us, and walked his way. We did not ask him his name or where he was coming from, neither did he ask us anything. Ajay and I had never talked about offering lifts to anybody before we started. It just happened. That journey of a few minutes was my first magical experience of Kumbha—how complete strangers come together to not only trust each other but also help each other. Meeting and moving together is what the Mela's *saṅgacchadhvam* spirit is all about.

Our destination in Kumbha Nagari was the *shivira* of my guru, Swami Ramabhadracharya. It was rather easy to find with several banners guiding us. On the way, I saw *shivira*s of almost every Hindu denomination and all major Hindu organizations. While there were many vehicles (they were allowed up to a specific distance from the bathing area), most of the people were on foot. It was a veritable ocean of humans—everybody who was outside the *shiviras* was moving somewhere, nobody was still. Mark Tully wrote about the 1989 Kumbha, "there was no panic, no pushing—just a slow, steady progress". The pilgrims I saw at the 2013 Kumbha were not much different, despite India having changed drastically in the preceding 24 years. There were solitary sadhus, couples, families with children, and large groups. By their attire, most of them appeared to be villagers. One could spot foreigners too. I started noticing the faces of the people. I saw hope, relief, happiness, piety, and gentleness, but I could not notice a single sad or gloomy face. In a place this crowded in Delhi or in the local trains of Mumbai, one is cautious and watchful—reflected in the way people guard their belongings and look at strangers with suspicion or mistrust. Here, I saw no caution, fear, or mistrust on the faces. It was like the whole Kumbha Nagari was one family, children of mother Ganga. And as children of a common mother, we were all there to move together—*saṅgacchadhvam*.

It was afternoon by the time we reached the *shivira*. It appeared like a basic historic tent from outside, but inside it was a modern makeshift accommodation with electricity, water supply, toilets, bathrooms, gas stove, TV cable connection, space for sleeping, a *katha pandal*, and a *yajna-shala*. Many people were staying inside like a large family. I paid obeisance to Guruji and other elders and met with people I had known for several years. In the afternoon, Guruji delivered a three-hour *katha* in the *katha pandal* on *Valmiki Ramayana*. He was accompanied by artists on the harmonium and the tabla. The *katha* started with a *kirtana* in which the audience participated and there were several bhajans and songs in between. Guruji explained the phrase *daśa-varṣa-sahasrāṇi daśa-varṣa-śatāni ca* in a verse of the *Valmiki Ramayana* as 33,000 years using the rules of Sanskrit grammar. I later came to know this was also the interpretation as per the *Tilaka* commentary. The three-hour *katha* ended with an *arati* followed by the following slogans, popularized by Karapatra Swami in the previous century:

> *dharma ki jaya ho,*
> *adharma ka nasha ho,*
> *praniyon mein sadbhavana ho,*
> *vishva ka kalyana ho,*
> *go-mata, ganga-mata, bharata-mata ki jaya ho*

"May *dharma* (the right path) be victorious. May *adharma* (the wrong path) be destroyed. May all living beings have benevolent feelings. May there be welfare of the whole world. Glory to mother cow, mother Ganga, and mother India (Bharata Mata)."

A fascinating thing about the Kumbha is that such *katha*s keep on taking place and are open to all. Listeners at the *katha* come and leave as they wish. Resources are willingly shared between organizations and even with small artiste troupes. In the evening, the same pandal was the stage of a lively and colourful *Rama Lila* performance by village artistes.

On the next day, 20 January, I sat for a few hours at a *havana* that was organized inside our *shivira*. There were several Shukla Yajur Veda pandits, most from Uttar Pradesh and some from Nepal, who were performing this group *havana*. Among them was Pt. Vachaspati Mishra, a scholar of Sanskrit between fifty and sixty years of age. He came to know that I could speak Sanskrit. We started a conversation. It was mostly in Sanskrit with some parts in Hindi. His Sanskrit was mellifluous and fluent. We talked about many topics—the Kumbha Mela, philosophical systems, various *sampradayas*, and contemporary Sanskrit authors and poets. I still remember parts of our Sanskrit conversation. He informed about his village, his joint family, his learning, his teaching, etc. We were two people very different in our background, education, and profession and yet we were seamlessly united by this divine festival of Kumbha Mela and the divine language Sanskrit.

In the afternoon, I witnessed the biggest *bhandara* I have ever seen in my life. Thousands, if not tens of thousands, of sadhus and pilgrims waited patiently on both sides of a large lane in the Kumbha Nagari. They were sitting on the ground in multiple lines with *donas* in front of them. News had spread that a big *bhandara* was being organized and many people had come for the lunch. I wondered if anybody could go hungry with so many organizations and individuals organizing distribution of free food for one and all during the entire duration of the Mela. This was the day when an affluent pilgrim was sponsoring a *bhandara*, hence the large scale. My evening was spent again listening to the Guruji's *katha*, roaming around, and talking with people.

In the evening Guruji spent some time answering questions from people. I asked him what the word *śubhaṃyu* (शुभंयु) in the second canto his epic *Shribhargavaraghaviyam* meant. He smiled and simply said, "*ahaṃśubhamoryus*" and then ordered that the next question be asked. I was taking down notes in a diary. It was only several days later that I understood that *ahaṃśubhamoryus* is the rule (5.2.140) in Panini's 'Ashtadhyayi' which explains how the word *śubhaṃyu* meaning "auspicious" is formed. Even five years later, I remember the question and the answer. This is an example of the learning people acquire at the Kumbha Mela by oral tradition, the traditional means of learning scriptural knowledge in India.

I was a witness to an unforgettable and moving event in the night. Guruji, who is without eyesight, has a special connection with the differently-abled. He often says, *"hain vikalanga maheshvara mere"* ("The differently-abled are the great lord for me"). Guruji never turns down a request from differently-abled persons, who in turn look up to him as a role model. Guruji had retired to bed after another long day in which numerous common people, sadhus, and saints had come to see him. A short while later, a dwarf pilgrim arrived at the *shivira* out of nowhere and said he wanted to meet Guruji. A volunteer went inside and woke up Guruji saying, *"Guruji, aapse milne ek bauna aaya hai"* ("Guruji, a dwarf has come to see you.") Guruji woke up immediately, sat down, and asked for him to be sent in. I went in along with a couple of volunteers. The dwarf pilgrim paid obeisance to Guruji. There was a short conversation during which Guruji asked where he had come from and how long he would be in Prayaga. I could see tears in the eyes of the dwarf who was elated beyond measure. Guruji blessed him and gave him fruits. He took leave of Guruji and vanished in the massive Mela crowd. Such are the numerous moving experiences one witnesses at the Kumbha Mela.

Monday, 21 January, was the day of leaving. Due to the extreme cold and a lack of opportunity, I had not yet taken a bath in the Sangama. But on the final day I decided I was not going back without experiencing what crores of pilgrims come to the Kumbha for. Around noon, I took leave of Guruji and the people at the *shivira*. I went along with Ajay to bathe in the Sangama. The car was not allowed beyond a point. We walked the remaining distance happily. The sun was shining brightly, making the cold bearable. There were uncountable people all around us, but nobody pushed. An equal number of people were walking towards the Sangama as were walking back after completing their *snana*. Now and then somebody would say *Ganga Maiya ki jaya* ("Glory to mother Ganga") or *Tirtharaja Prayaga ki jaya* ("Glory to Prayaga, the king of sacred places"). The energy and enthusiasm were enchantingly infectious. There was nobody in the unending ocean of people that I knew apart from Ajay, and yet I felt inside me that I know all of them—we are all connected in our faith and our reverence towards our common mother, goddess Ganga. Finally, we reached the river. We waded till we reached waist deep waters. I took three dips, prayed to Surya, and then just stood in the water with closed eyes and folded hands. As a small child confesses to its mother, I silently confessed, "Mother, I have sinned so much in this life and I do not deserve it, but please forgive me if you can." Tears rolled down from my eyes then. Tears roll down my eyes as I write this, five years later. Time stood still for those few minutes I was in the water. I felt it was just me and mother Ganga—I found solitude and peace right in the midst of a massive crowd and a continuous din. I experienced the Kumbha Mela internally and externally at the same time. It was not one of the sacred bathing dates, but it was my very own sacred moment with mother Ganga at the Prayaga Kumbha.

As Ajay and I were about to start our return journey from

Prayaga to Lucknow, a sadhu from our *shivira* stopped us and asked, "Where are you going?" I responded, "Lucknow." He said, "I have to go to Haridwar, can you drop me at the train station in Lucknow?" I said, "Why not? Please come in." And he entered with his small bag and *kamandalu*. He was nearly bald, with only some white hair left at the back of his head which was neatly tied into a *shikha*. The *urdhvapundra* on his forehead gave away his Ramanandi Vaishnava identity. He wore a long white beard with a thick moustache on his face, *mudras* on both arms and chest, a sacred thread across his upper body, a *dhoti* below, and wooden slippers in his feet. His name was Raghuvara Dasa ("servant of the best among Raghus", i.e. "servant of Rama"). All his belongings fit in a small bag. He had a smiling persona and appeared like a doting grandfather. The journey started. We talked for a while. In the Indian tradition, we are not supposed to ask sadhus and *samnyasis* about their former (*purvashrama*) life, and I took care about this in our conversations, entirely in Hindi.

Usually when I travel, I keep my music collection on my phone or handheld device. More often than not, I end up listening to Pt. Chhannulal Mishra, whose musical virtuosity is equally matched by his profound *bhava* (emotion) and clear pronunciation. Just as I was about to start playing his tracks with my earphones on, Raghuvara Dasa took out an old copy of the *Sundarakanda* of Tulasidasa's *Ramacharitamanasa*, and started singing verses from it in a low voice. Having heard the abridged rendition of the *Sundarakanda* by Mukesh and the unabridged rendition by Pt. Chhannulal Mishra many times, I can recite many of its verses from my memory. I started singing along with Raghuvara Dasa in the same tune and tempo he was singing. He was delighted to find another singer and we sang the whole *kanda* together on our way to Lucknow. This was live music with a *bairagi* sadhu, something I had never imagined I would experience. It was all made possible by the *saṅgacchadhvam* spirit of the Kumbha Mela which had still not left us, though we had left the Kumbha Nagari hours ago.

On the way to Lucknow, we were stuck in a slow-moving and long traffic jam for nearly half an hour. I worried I might miss my flight to Mumbai and the connecting flight to Hong Kong. As we had to rush, we could not drop Raghuvara Dasa at the railway station. We dropped him at Telibagh and requested a tempo-driver to drop him at the railway station. I reached the airport just in time. Two of my uncles had arrived there to meet me. After a quick meeting, I rushed inside. When I took off my jacket and placed it along with my bag for the X-ray check, a CISF personnel noted the sand on my jacket and bag. Out of curiosity, he asked where so much sand came from. I told him I was just coming from the Kumbha Mela. He asked me in Hindi, "How is it? I think I must go." I replied in Hindi, "I have never experienced anything better in the world. You must certainly go." He replied, "Now I will certainly go." We smiled at each other as I proceeded to board my flight.

Nashik: 2015

During the 2015 Nashik-Tryambakeshwar Kumbha, I was living in Mumbai. Life had changed a lot since 2013. My ex-wife and I had separated earlier that year: an unfortunate but unavoidable event. I fought the tough time by writing the book *Mahaviri: Hanuman-Chalisa Demystified*, an expanded and annotated English translation of Guruji's *Mahaviri* commentary on the *Hanuman-Chalisa*. The book was published in August by my family's publishing house when the Mela started. I wanted to present the first copy to Guruji, who was camping at the Mela. I had found company in Apurv Agarwal, a *gurubhrata* in Mumbai who also wanted to visit the Mela. We planned a weekend trip to Nashik. Most hotels were running full, but we could book Hotel Palms Residency at New Adgoan Naka.

We set out on the morning of 5 September, the day of Janmasthami. The road journey from Mumbai to Nashik was very smooth, thanks to the excellent condition of the Mumbai-Nashik road. We reached Nashik around 10 am. The city was much more developed than I thought it would be, there was a large residential complex, Samraat Vrindavan, with lawns and amenities right next to our hotel. After checking in, we headed to the Mela. In Prayaga, the temporary megacity is built on the large sandy river beds which are exposed when the water recedes after the monsoons, and there are no permanent constructions next to what becomes the main bathing area during the Kumbha. Nashik was different—most of the temporary *shiviras* here were spread out over a larger area and many were located next to permanent, metalled roads. There are permanent constructions and metalled roads even next to the main bathing ghat at Rama Kunda. As we passed the Nashik *sadhugrama*, we saw the impressive Jagadguru Ramanandacharya Pravesha-dvara welcoming the Kumbha pilgrims. This massive and beautiful arch with hanging bells and saffron flags had been inaugurated just a few days ago in the presence of Swami Narendracharya (a Ramanandi saint in Maharashtra), Gyan Das, (Mahant of Hanumangarhi,

Ayodhya), Amit Shah (President of the BJP), and Devendra Fadnavis (Chief Minister of Maharashtra).

We reached Guruji's *shivira* around noon and I presented the first copy of the book to him. A *katha* on the *Ramacharitamanasa* started soon. Many local residents and people from nearby villages had come to listen. This being Maharashtra, Guruji sang a few Marathi devotional songs, much to the delight of the Marathi-speakers in the audience. In the evening, we saw a distinguished saint paying visit to Guruji. Lakshmiprapanna Jeeyar Swami, a *shishya* of the late Tridandi Swami Vishvaksenacharya, had come to invite Guruji to deliver a *katha* on *Valmiki Ramayana* during the *sahasrabdi mahotsava* (1000th birth anniversary) of Ramanujacharya, the propounder of the *Vishishtadvaita* philosophy. Though the celebrations were planned for late 2017, preparations were already on. Jeeyar Swami and Guruji then discussed several matters related to *dharma* and social service. Such meetings between sadhus and saints to discuss contemporary matters and coordinate their efforts continue to be one of the main objectives of the Kumbha Melas.

The evening was live with Janmasthami celebrations at Nashik. The numerous Vaishnava organizations present at the Kumbha Mela joined *tirthayatris* in celebrating the festival with great fervour at midnight.

Meanwhile, word had spread in the day that the ABAP was not satisfied with the bathing arrangements as *tirthayatris* had to walk a long distance to reach the bathing ghats on the first *shahi snana* day. Narendra Giri (president, ABAP) and Chidananda Sarasvati (Paramartha Niketana Ashram) spoke with the media and requested the Chief Minister for better *vyavastha* (arrangements), including more buses for *tirthayatris* and closer drops to the ghats.

The next morning Apurv and I went for the bath at Rama Kunda, the venue of the *shahi snana* at Nashik. Rama Kunda, literally "the reservoir of Rama", was built by Chitrarao Khatarkar in 1696 CE. It is believed to be the bathing spot of Lord Rama and Mother Sita, hence the name. Unlike the Ganga at the Sangama in Prayaga, the Godavari is very narrow at Rama Kunda—only around 25 metres wide. The river bed at Rama Kunda had been concretized during the 2003 Kumbha Mela at Nashik. We took the dip in the presence of many other *tirthayatris*. We hardly knew that barely seven months later, Rama Kunda would run dry for the first time in 139 years due to a severe drought. While the bathing ghat and the number of *tirthayatris* was much smaller compared to Prayaga in 2013, the spirit was as lively. I noticed a higher proportion of *tirthayatris* from South India as compared to the Prayaga Kumbha. In the afternoon, Apurv and I took leave of Guruji and came back to Mumbai.

I remember the Nashik Kumbha for a serendipitous chain of events that started on 6 September in Nashik. Around 11 am, two middle-aged South Indian couples from Mumbai arrived to have a *darshan* of Guruji. They were highly-educated people who had come to their first Kumbha. They heard Guruji was camping at the Mela and came to see him. As they were waiting, they came to know we had also travelled from Mumbai. A conversation started soon. The visitors were very pleased to learn about Guruji's literary works in Sanskrit and Hindi. They asked if any of his works was translated into English. I showed them a copy of my translation of the *Mahaviri*. One of the gentlemen, Sitapathi Ganesh, asked me if he could get two signed copies. I said I did not have two, but took down his contact details. My family's publishing house e-mailed him a few days later. He requested for two signed copies, one for "Kamala and Ganesh" to be sent to a Mumbai address and another to "Ramanathan and Lalitha" to be sent to a Chennai address. I gladly signed the books which were soon dispatched. A few weeks later, I received a phone call from a Chennai landline number. The voice at the other end said, "This is Ramanathan Krishnan, tennis player." Before I could realize what was happening, he said "Thanks for sending me your book, I loved reading it". It then struck me that the Ramanathan in Chennai who I had signed my book for was none other than Ramanathan Krishnan, a two-time Wimbledon semi-finalist and one of India's most successful tennis players. It turned out he had got my number from Sitapathi Ganesh, who is his brother-in-law. Some days later I connected with Ramanathan Krishnan's son Ramesh Krishnan; in 1993, I had watched him defeat Rodolphe Gilbert to complete India's spectacular victory over France in the Davis Cup. At my request, Krishnan junior sent me a photo of the father and son with the book. The Kumbha Mela is an amazing place where complete strangers meet and walk a few steps together, like Sitapathi Ganesh and I did at the Nashik Kumbha.

Ujjain: 2016

The beginning of the year 2016 was momentous. On 20 January, I officially became a single parent: I got divorced from my ex-wife in Bengaluru, ending a major life chapter. I had the custody of both my children and though I had the continued support of my parents, I had still not come to terms with the challenges of single parenting. I was very sad and nothing was helping. When the month-long Simhastha Kumbha started in Ujjain on 22 April, I thought perhaps visiting the Mela would help my mood. My children were too young to accompany me, so I planned a weekend trip on 30 April and 1 May. As luck would have it, Doordarshan News decided to telecast my interview on the *Varttavali* weekly Sanskrit news magazine on 30 April with a repeat telecast on 1 May, which meant I would miss watching the feature in all probability. There was not much to think—the experience of the Simhastha Kumbha Mela was worth missing watching my first appearance on national media.

I took the 6.30 am Jet Airways flight from Mumbai to the Devi Ahilya Bai Holkar Airport at Indore on 30 April. On the flight I met a father-son duo, also travelling to Ujjain to attend the Mela. The son was a businessman in Mumbai who had returned to India after working in the US for eighteen years. He was excited to travel to his first Kumbha. I had planned to travel to Ujjain with Anshul Gupta, a good friend and a fellow IIM Bangalore graduate from Indore who was then serving in the Indian Police Service (IPS). After I landed at Indore, Anshul called to inform that he would not be able to make it that day. I took a taxi from the airport to travel alone to Ujjain. Like the Mumbai-Nashik road I had taken seven months earlier, the road from Indore to Ujjain was in an excellent condition. Large banners and hoardings welcoming *tirthayatris* to the Mela were placed at regular intervals, starting from the airport.

I reached Ujjain, the city of Mahakala, around 9.30 am. The

heat was already unbearable. Having attended two Kumbha Melas earlier, the people around appeared quite familiar. This would be the biggest Simhastha Kumbha ever, with an estimated five crore pilgrims. The arrangements were very impressive. There were loudspeakers at regular intervals making announcements. Manned information centres were present every few hundred metres—all one needed to ask was where a particular *shivira* was and the personnel would help with its precise location and directions. While I did not have a chance to take a bath in the Shipra this time, I was informed by Apurv Agarwal (who visited the Mela a few days later) that a child who fell in the river was saved within ten seconds by lifeguards on duty in front of his eyes.

It took some time to find Guruji's *shivira* in Mangalanatha Zone. By the time I reached there, the programme of the day had started. This time it was a nine-day *parayana* of the *Ramacharitamanasa*. On each day there would be two sessions with a small break in between for resting. Led by Guruji and the musicians on stage, around two hundred people in the pandal were singing Tulasidasa's immortal verses. After every few *dohas*, the musicians would change the *raga* for the next set of *chaupais* and the people in the pandal would follow. The mercury soon soared to 40°C around noon but failed to melt the spirit of the singers. The day's programme ended around 12.30 pm. In the afternoon, Guruji wanted to listen to the *Mantra Ramayana*, a brilliant Sanskrit work by Nilakantha Chaturdhara, the famous commentator on the *Mahabharata*. I volunteered to read, and though not many visitors understood what was being read, people kept coming and going paying respects to Guruji and bowing down to him without disturbing him. I have experienced at several large religious gatherings in India that people know how to pay obeisance to sadhus or saints without disturbing them.

While going back from the *shivira* to my hotel near the Ujjain railway station, I shared an e-rickshaw with two local residents of Ujjain—a septuagenarian old man and his six-year-old sweet granddaughter. The girl started a conversation with me. She asked me, "*Aap kahan se aaye ho*?" (Where have you come from?) I responded, "Mumbai." She shot back with her next question, "*Aapke Mumbai mein bhi Simhastha hota hai*?" (Does the Simhastha take place in your Mumbai also?) I smiled, her grandfather laughed. I told her with a sad face, "*Naheen hota, beta, isiliye yahan aaye hain*." (No, it does not, child, that is why I am here). The girl then started asking me some riddles and the conversation went on to her school, her friends, what she likes to eat and so on. The fact that she was almost my daughter's age made the conversation even more memorable. The girl's grandfather proudly told me that he was seventy-five years old and it was the seventh Simhastha of his life. He said he had never seen such big crowds. He then said his only desire was to live to witness his ninth Simhastha, as his late father had. I prayed that it will happen. The grandfather and granddaughter got down at their stop. I bid goodbye to them. I did not ask their names, I do not remember their faces very well, and I will most probably never meet them in my life again. However, I will remember the experience of the short journey I made with them for a long time to come. The three of us came together at the Kumbha Mela and moved together on a common path—*saṅgacchadhvam* again.

On the next morning, when I reached the *shivira*, word was

abuzz that the Chief Minister (CM), Shivraj Singh Chouhan, was about to visit our *shivira* with his wife, Sadhana Singh. There were several phone calls between the volunteers at the *shivira* and the personal secretary to the CM. It appeared the CM had decided to take a surprise tour of the Kumbha Nagara to take stock of the arrangements and administration at the Mela. Arrangements were made in our *shivira* for welcoming him. After several delays, ostensibly due to traffic congestion, they finally arrived in the afternoon. Guruji was sitting on a bed, and a sofa had been arranged for Chouhan and his wife to sit. To my surprise, the couple chose to sit below on the carpet, close to Guruji's feet. There were no armed guards and there was no large contingent either—just a couple of unarmed bodyguards in safari suits with the couple in our *shivira*. The room was quite hot despite an air-conditioner working, but somehow the couple did not care. The couple gifted a shawl and a coconut to Guruji and enquired about the arrangements at the Mela. Guruji praised the arrangements at the Mela. When the CM asked what else he could do, Guruji asked him to develop further the Maharishi Panini Sanskrit Evam Vedic Vishwavidyalaya in Ujjain, the city of Kalidasa. Before leaving the *shivira*, the CM and his wife spent some time to take a look at the exhibition of paintings made by differently-abled students in our *shivira*.

I later came to know that the CM also visited Swami Sharanananda of the Karshni Ashram, Avadheshananda Giri of the Juna Akhara, and Narendra Giri of the Niranjani Akhara on the same day. Just a few days later, the CM would be back once again at Simhastha Kumbha, this time to oversee the relief and restoration work after seven people were killed in the Mela by a deadly thunderstorm on the night of 5 May.

Late afternoon, I left back for Indore along with Sanjay Chaturvedi, a *gurubhrata* who had come from Nagpur and was also headed to Indore. We reached a spot where the road was elevated as we exited the Mela area. From here, we had a most amazing sight of pilgrims taking the *Pancha-kosi Yatra*. This is an annual pilgrimage in which pilgrims perform the *parikrama* of Ujjain. The *yatris* walk nearly 120 km over six days in the sweltering heat when temperatures soar above 40°C. Usually, the *yatra* starts on the tenth day of the dark half of the *Vaishakha* month and ends on the new moon day. This year, it had begun two days earlier as lakhs of people were expected to perform the *yatra* in the year of the Simhastha. As far as I could see, I saw men, women, and children walking slowly. Most of the adults had their belongings on their head. The saris of different colours shone brightly as the sun was going down. These pilgrims would walk around 24 km every day, circumambulating Ujjain and visiting twenty-eight *tirthas* before resting on the banks of mother Shipra. I was reminded of the *kalpavasi*s of the Prayaga Kumbha in 2013. The location was different and the weather was very different, but the faith, the endurance, the hope, and the bliss of the pilgrims was the same. Another thing was same here: the underlying spirit of *sangacchadhvam*—meeting and moving together.

As I waited at the Indore airport for my 9.15 pm return flight to Mumbai, I was already feeling much better. The experience of the two days had made me forget all my worries. Perhaps it was yet another experience of the Kumbha Mela or perhaps it was the sight of the resolute *tirthayatris* undertaking the *Pancha-kosi Yatra* under the burning sun, but I had this feeling in my mind that life has to move ahead, no matter how burning our sorrows are. Those two days had made me come out of my gloominess of months. I returned to Mumbai rejuvenated and reinvigorated. I was to soon come out of my depression. And as luck would have it, Doordarshan News would put up my interview, which I had missed watching live, on YouTube four days later.

Prayaga: 2019

I was back at the Prayaga Ardha Kumbha in 2019. This time, many more friends and colleagues travelled to the Mela. As there were few flights to the newly upgraded Prayagraj airport, I chose to fly to Lucknow from Mumbai. I reached Lucknow at around 10 pm on Friday, 15 September. Having left the Lucknow airport in a taxi at around 10.30 pm, I reached the Kumbha Nagari in Prayaga at around 2.30 am. Even in the biting cold, there were policemen all around to help visitors reach their destination. With their help, I could easily find the tent in Ganga Sankul, sector 19, Arail Ghat.

On the next morning, the Kumbha Nagari was engulfed by a dense fog till around eight. When the fog cleared, I decided to walk the 3-km distance to the Sangama area along the Sankatmochan Marg, which runs parallel to the Ganga downstream of the Sangama. The best way to experience the Kumbha, especially the one in Prayaga, is by walking. The first thing I realized was that this Ardha Kumbha was clearly bigger than the 2013 Kumbha. The diversity seen in a stretch of 3 km was unparalleled. A stall named Food Plaza Meghalaya was selling vegetarian food from Northeast India. A large camp named Sanskriti Gram was set up by the Uttar Pradesh Tourism Department to showcase the culture of the state. It had been inaugurated by the Chief Minister on 10 January, before the Mela began. Cows and calves roamed freely. Water taps had been put up at regular distances by the Uttar Pradesh Jal Nigam. A lonely sadhu outside a *shivira* was singing bhajans in ecstasy. He readily posed for a few photos on my request. Milk distribution centres dotted the road. I spotted several *swachhagrahis*, identifiable by the text on their jackets, walking. An *anna-kshetra* was serving free breakfast to one and all. An old couple was walking patiently, symbolizing the togetherness of the wife and the husband in life and death. The man, looking much older, was barefoot and needed the woman's support to walk. A camp belonged to the uniquely named Pagaldas Maharaj. An ochre-robed sadhu with just the basic belongings, including a *kamandalu*, walked past. Another Vaishnava sadhu was busy on his mobile phone. A *shivira* housed a temporary office of the Uttar Pradesh Home Guards. A young girl was selling flowers and articles for Puja near the Sangama. I spotted a large tubewell put up by the Uttar Pradesh Jal Nigam. At another place in sector 19, several water tankers were stationed near the office of the Uttar Pradesh Jal Nigam. The social organizations present were as diverse as one could imagine: from the *Akhil Bharatiya Khatri Mahasabha* to the *Akhil Bharatiya Kanyakubja Vaishya Sabha*. Kali Baba Maharaja had come all the way from Kamakhya Peetha, Assam. A camp by Jaya Shri Mahakala Seva Trust had a goal of making 11.25 lakh Shivalingas of clay by Shivaratri, which fell on 4 March in 2019. A group of *kalpavasis* was distributing free bananas to all passers-by. Garbage pick-up vans ensured that the Mela area was largely clean. A hunchbacked old woman *kalpavasi* was walking barefoot, all alone. With so much government spending, it was not a surprise to see the office of the director of the Local Fund Audit Department in the Mela area. All this and much more makes one truly appreciate the unimaginable scale and diversity of the Kumbha Mela.

Many brands were present at the Ardha Kumbha in 2019. LG had installed a stall in sector 19 with washing machines for free use. Outside the Prayagraj Mela Authority office in sector 19, LG had installed water purifiers for free drinking water. Hamam had sponsored many changing rooms near the Sangama. JCB was advertizing on banners promoting cleanliness. Banks and financial firms were omnipresent. The luxurious tent city in sector 20 had a temporary HDFC Bank ATM and a Muthoot Finance centre. Syndicate Bank had not only an ATM but a fully-fledged branch in sector 19. Temporary mobile charging ATMs showed the extent of digital revolution in India. NTPC Limited had a small exhibition centre. Ultratech Cement had sponsored informational banners at one of the many police help centres, while Vodafone was advertising the need to stay connected at a computerized lost and found centre.

There were elaborate arrangements to deal with all kinds of situations. There were many police chowkis and help centres, including some near the pontoon bridges. A temporary hospital was set up in sector 19 with an ambulance stationed for free medical care and emergency response. Not far from this hospital, the AYUSH Department had set up a homeopathic clinic. A medical treatment camp was set up by the Air Force Station Bamrauli. All bathing ghats were barricaded. At just a little distance from the shores of the rivers, there were large floats in orange colour to prevent people from venturing deep into the water. I saw boats of the National Disaster Response Force at the Sangama, on the south side of the Yamuna, and a boat ambulance operated by the NDRF. There were floating boat lane dividers to manage the boat traffic. The movement of the boats was organized and regulated: even the direction in which the boats moved was fixed. There were *shivira*s of the Flood Relief Force, which comes under the Uttar Pradesh Provincial Armed Constabulary. Sector 20 had a *shivira* of the Uttar Pradesh State Disaster Response Force. This camp was set up on the lines of the NDRF camps to deal with disasters. There was a riot control vehicle, a Rapid Mobile 207 Vajra, at the Sangama area. I saw a group of armed Border Security Force (BSF) personnel in sector 19. Many fire control centres with fire vehicles were present. There were *shivira*s of the Allahabad High Court on both the south side and the north side of the Yamuna. Even the Food Safety and Standards Authority of India (FSSAI) was present with a mobile food testing camp.

On the afternoon of Saturday, my colleague Anirudh Somani and his sister Radhika Jain joined me for experiencing the Mela. It was their first experience of a Kumbha Mela. I met them at the tent city in sector 20 and we went to the Vishva Sahabhagita Kshetra on the south side of the Yamuna. After clicking some photos, we had lunch at the Sangama area. There is no dearth of options for food in the Kumbha for those who pay. Food without onion and garlic is also easy to get. For those who do not or cannot pay, free food is available at hundreds of places. As we were finishing our lunch, the Sangama area suddenly became crowded. We came to know that the Vice President of India, M. Venkaiah Naidu, was visiting the Mela.

Due to such VIP movements, car traffic was extremely slow and it was much easier to just walk to the nearest ghat and cross the rivers on foot.

We decided to take a boat to the Sangama for the biggest experience of the Prayaga Kumbha: the *snana* at the confluence of the Ganga and the Yamuna. Two boatmen, who wore T-shirts sponsored by a brand, helped us and other visitors sit in a boat one by one. These hard-working boatmen shoulder one of the biggest responsibilities of the Kumbha at Prayaga: ferrying the devout from the shores of the rivers to the sacred Sangama. Life jackets were compulsory: they could be taken off only for the bath in the shallow waters of the Sangama. The boatmen knew the exact depth of the water in feet at all places. For the discerning pilgrims, they pointed out the place where the Yamuna meets the Ganga: the colour of the water current changes suddenly from bluish green (water of the Yamuna) to muddy (water of the Ganga).

At the main bath area close to the Sangama, tens of boats were stationed. Hundreds of people were offering their prayers and experiencing solace amidst the din as they dipped themselves in the holy waters. Men and women, children and the aged, all were together in the care of mother Ganga. After the Sangama *snana*, our boat dropped us to the north of the Yamuna near Akbar's Fort. Here, life was abuzz as in a busy Indian metro. The worlds of spirituality and worldly life came together seamlessly. Many panda camps, with their unique flags, were present. Boards displayed verses from scriptures extolling the greatness of Prayaga. The Indian Army had two camps on the north side of the Yamuna for serving personnel and ex-servicemen. Most banners mentioned only Kumbha, as the fair was branded by the government. I found one which clearly mentioned Ardha Kumbha. Near the entry to Akbar's Fort, which houses the Akshay Vat and Patalpuri Mandir, was a small market. A street-side book vendor was selling religious and spiritual books. As one would expect, most titles were popular scriptures like the *Ramacharitamanasa*, the *Bhagavad-Gita*, the *Bhagavata-Purana*, etc., by Gita Press. I was pleased to see some rare books like *Karmathaguru*. Near the bookstall, ISKCON volunteers were distributing free copies of their books.

Anirudh and Radhika wanted to visit the *akharas* to see sadhus and camps of various *akharas*. I took a boat back to the south of the Yamuna. After sunset, boats stop ferrying people and one has to cross the rivers either on foot or in a vehicle using the pontoon bridges. Disembarking on the south of the Yamuna, I saw a multilingual sign in English, Hindi, Telugu, Tamil, and Bengali. Many such signs featuring multiple Indian languages were put up in both the Kumbha Nagari and the city by the authorities. I reached my tent at the Ganga Sankul in sector 19. In the evening, several readers came to get signed copies of the first edition of this book. I signed copies for Prashant Mishra, who came with his family, and Manish Sand, who came all the way from Varanasi. In the evening, my friend and *gurubhrata* Manishkumar Shukla from Bengaluru and his parents from Kanpur joined me at the Ganga Sankul. Shortly thereafter, Pushkar Sharma, who I had first met a few months ago, called me unexpectedly. He had come to know from my Facebook posts that I was at the Mela. Pushkar invited me to meet Swami Chidananda Saraswati to present him my book on Kumbha. Manishkumar and I went to the beautiful Paramartha Niketana camp and were very pleased to meet

Swami Chidananda Saraswati and present a copy of my book. I gifted book copies to several other readers. The Mela connects people in many such ways.

The next day, 17 February, I went for another Sangama *snana*, this time with Manishkumar and his parents. The morning was clear with no fog at all, though the water was quite cold and it soon became so cloudy that the morning sun appeared like the moon in the evening. After the *snana*, Manishkumar and his parents soon took leave and left for Kanpur. Every day of the Kumbha Mela comes with new experiences. During every *snana*, one experiences bliss by just listening to the waves of the Yamuna and the Ganga.

Anirudh, Radhika and I had hired a taxi to return to Lucknow, from where we had to fly back to Mumbai on the same flight. However, we were stuck in massive traffic jams as we exited the Kumbha Nagari. Traffic policemen were diverting traffic in different directions to avoid any further build-ups. We got tense that we would miss our flight, and at one point, Anirudh hilariously proposed that we avail of the helicopter service, which was being offered at the Mela as part of adventure tourism, to get out of Prayagraj. We lost several hours due to the traffic jams and missed our flight. We booked the flight for the next day and spent the night in Lucknow at Anirudh and Radhika's relatives' place. The next day, while playing a game of chess with Anirudh on our flight to Mumbai, I reminisced about my nearly perfect experience of the 2019 Ardha Kumbha: it had ended with the loss of one day but the gain of a lifetime's worth of memories.

Concluding Remarks

Except for the Haridwar Kumbha, I have attended all the other three Kumbha Melas and the Ardha Kumbha at Prayaga. I have also visited Haridwar several times in my life and I am sure I will experience the Haridwar Kumbha Mela also one day. There are many differences in the four places and the melas held at these places and yet I have found that the collaborative and inclusive Hindu values of *saṅgacchadhvam* and *vasudhaiva kuṭumbakam* ("the earth alone is the family") are the same. The experiences I had at the four melas were quite different, but the inner bliss that I have felt as a result of those experiences is the same. My personal experiences of the different Kumbha Melas are dissimilar and yet similar, quite like the diverse traditions and people present at the Kumbha Mela.

12. Kumbha 2025

The 2025 Prayaga Kumbha, being branded as a Maha Kumbha, will be held from 13 January to 26 February. The sacred bathing dates will be *Pausha Purnima* (13 January), *Makara Sankranti* (14 January), *Mauni Amavasya* (29 January), *Vasanta Panchami* (3 February), *Maghi Purnima* (12 February), and *Maha Shivaratri* (26 March). The motto for the Mela is *sarva-siddhi-pradaḥ kumbhaḥ*, meaning "Kumbha is the bestower of all accomplishments."

The logo of the 2025 Kumbha.

Bigger Than Ever Before

The size and scope of the 2025 Kumbha will be bigger than any Kumbha Mela ever. An estimated 40 crore people are expected to visit the Kumbha Mela in 2025. Some estimates put the number even higher, at 50 crore. In contrast, an estimated 24 crore people visited the Ardha Kumbha Mela in 2019 and 12 crore visited the Kumbha in 2013. Around 6 crore people are expected to be at the Mela on Mauni Amavasya (29 January), the biggest bathing day. The number of visitors at the Mela on Mauni Amavasya in 2013 was 3 crore and that in 2019 was 5 crore. About 250 flights, 1,000 trains, 7,000 buses and 20 lakh private vehicles are expected to enter Prayagraj on the Mauni Amavasya day. The budget for organizing the 2025 Kumbha is Rs 6,382 crore. This is more than 50% higher than the budget of the Ardha Kumbha in 2019 (Rs 4,200 crore) and more than six times the budget of the Kumbha in 2013. In addition to government spending, around Rs 3,000 crore is expected to be spent by India Inc. on branding and marketing during the Mela.

The area designated for the Mela is 5,000 hectares, up from 3,200 hectares for the 2019 Ardha Kumbha and 2,000 hectares for the 2013 Kumbha. The Kumbha Mela area has been notified as a temporary new district, the 76th one, of Uttar Pradesh for a period of four months. This district will have 66 villages and 4 tehsils. The Kumbha Nagari will have 25 sectors, up from 20 in 2019 and 14 in 2013. Thirty pontoon bridges will be constructed over the Ganga and the Yamuna, up from 22 in 2019.

What's New at the 2025 Kumbha?

This edition of the Kumbha Mela is being envisaged as a *Surkashit* (safe), *Swacch* (clean), *Sugam* (accessible), and *Sanskritik* (cultural) Kumbha. The famous Nagvasuki Temple has been renovated for the Kumbha Mela. The new structure combines traditional Hindu architecture with modern elements. A new corridor has been constructed at the Akshayvat Temple to provide easy access to the temple. To regulate the flow of devotees, entry to this corridor will be allowed in batches. The Lord Hanuman corridor, on the other hand, will allow hassle-free entry to the devotees owing to enough space inside the corridor. The Lete Hue Hanuman Mandir has also been developed. A state-of-the-art Convention and Cultural Centre will host discourses, performances, and exhibitions. There is emphasis on making the Kumbha plastic-free. A water sports arena and floating jetties have been planned to provide recreation facilities at the Kumbha.

As many as 201 road widening and strengthening projects have been carried out. Forty junctions and 48 roads have been beautified. One hundred and one parking areas have assigned. Fourteen Roads Over Bridge (ROBs) and flyovers have been constructed.

The digital footprint will be higher in Kumbha 2025. More than 1.5 lakh tentage and toilets will be monitored. Around 2,600 crowd-monitoring cameras will be set up. More than 10 drone-based surveillance and disaster management centres will be operational. There will be 10 fully digital lost and found centres.

Like in the 2019 Ardha Kumbha, there will be focus on

water, sanitation, and hygiene. The Uttar Pradesh Jal Nigam has laid around 1,250 km of water pipelines to feed around 200 water ATMs and 85 water booths. In the 2019 Ardha Kumbha, the length of water pipelines was 1,050 km and there were far fewer water ATMs and water booths. Around 1.5 lakh toilets have been constructed. More than 25,000 dustbins have been installed in the Mela area. Around 15,000 sanitation workers, including Ganga Seva Doots, will be tasked with keeping the Mela area clean. In addition, more than 160 waste management vehicles will be on duty. More than 3 lakh saplings have been planted to make the Kumbha more green.

The infrastructure around the rivers and elsewhere has also been upgraded. Sixteen ghats have been renovated and developed. Thirteen temples and corridors have been renovated. Twelve temporary ghats have been created. Around 8 km of riverfront roads have been laid.

The largest temporary city in the world will have more than one lakh tents in the Mela area. More than 69,000 LED lights (as against 40,700 in 2019) and solar hybrid street lights will be installed. Around 400 km of temporary roads will be constructed using chequered plates.

This Kumbha will be more digital than the previous Melas. A first-ever AI-powered chatbot named Kumbh Saha'AI'yak has been launched. Powered by Bhavish Aggarwal-led Krutrim, Kumbh Saha'AI'yak will be a 24/7 digital companion for visitors. The chatbot will be available in many languages including Hindi, English, Tamil, Telugu, Marathi, Malayalam, Urdu, Gujarati, Punjabi, Kannada, and Bengali and will offer several user-friendly interfaces with clickable options, voice commands, and media-enriched content. AI-enabled CCTV cameras will keep a watch on each of the 30 pontoon bridges. In case of an emergency or a possibility of overloading, the CCTV cameras will send a warning to the Integrated Command and Control Centre. The Kumbha will also be more digitally accessible than ever. News 18 has launched News18 Kumbh, a new YouTube channel, to provide exclusive coverage of the Kumbha Mela.

Concluding Remarks

By all imaginable measures, the 2025 Kumbha at Prayaga will be the largest Kumbha Mela ever. It will be more Indian and more global than ever before. Be it cross-department coordination; the confluence of literature, arts, and music; infrastructure upgrades; connectivity by air, land, or water; inclusivity; cleanliness; digital footprint; corporate involvement; or eco-friendliness—the Mela will set unprecedented standards. The traditional Mela will become more modern and its *saṅgacchadhvam* spirit will prevail, bringing people together yet again.

Appendix

Verses chanted during *kalasha* worship

A translation of the below verses was provided in the first chapter.

कलशस्य मुखे विष्णुः कण्ठे रुद्रः समाश्रितः ।
मूले त्वस्य स्थितो ब्रह्मा मध्ये मातृगणाः स्थिताः ॥
कुक्षौ तु सागराः सर्वे सप्तद्वीपा वसुन्धरा ।
ऋग्वेदोऽथ यजुर्वेदः सामवेदो ह्यथर्वणः ।
अङ्गैश्च सहिताः सर्वे कलशं तु समाश्रिताः ॥

The Puranic origin of Kumbha Mela

The following verses, a translation of which is presented in the first chapter, are attributed to the *Skanda Purana*. The versions below are based on the Gita Press publication *Mahakumbha-parva* and the website of the Jagadguru Ashrama, a Nimbarka organization based in Nepal. There are some differences in the two versions. I have attempted to provide the more logical reading in case of such differences.

अथातः संप्रवक्ष्यामि कलशोत्पत्तिमुत्तमाम् ।
उत्तरे हिमवत्पार्श्वे क्षीरोदो नाम सागरः ॥
आरब्धं मन्थनं तत्र देवैर्दानवपूर्वकैः ।
मन्थानं मन्दरं कृत्वा नेत्रं कृत्वा तु वासुकिम् ॥
मूले कूर्मन्तु संस्थाप्य विष्णोर्बाहू च मन्दरे ।
एकत्र देवताः सर्वे बलिमुख्यास्तथैकतः ॥

मथ्यमाने तदा तस्मिन् क्षीरोदे सागरोत्तमे।
उत्पन्नं गरलं पूर्वं शम्भुना भक्षितं च तत्॥
अथ स्वास्थ्यं गते लोके प्रकथ्यन्तेऽद्य तानि हि।
उत्पन्नानि च रत्नानि यानि तत्र महान्ति च॥
विमानं पुष्पकं पूर्वमुत्तमं हंसवाहनम्।
नाग ऐरावतश्चैव पादप: पारिजातक:॥
वीणावाद्यान्तरं चैव रम्भा नृत्यगुणन्विता।
मणिरत्नं कौस्तुभाख्यं बालचन्द्रस्तथैव च॥
कुण्डलानि धनुश्चैव गाव: पञ्च शिवास्तथा।
लक्ष्मी: सुरूपा यमुना सुशीला सुरभिस्तथा॥
उच्चै:श्रवा: समुत्पन्नो लक्ष्मीश्च वरवर्णिनी।
तथा धन्वन्तरिर्देवो विश्वकर्मा कलाविद:॥
कलशश्च समुद्भूतो धन्वन्तरिकरोल्लसन्।
मुखान्तं सुधया पूर्ण: सर्वेषां हि मनोहर:॥
अजितस्य पदाम्भोजकृपयैव समुद्धृतम्।
क्षीराब्धिलोडनोद्भूतं कलशं दिव्यरत्नकम्॥
दृष्ट्वा तु तत्क्षणादेव महाबलपराक्रम:।
जयन्तोऽमृतमादाय गतो देवप्रचोदित:॥
देवकर्मसमालोच्य तदा दैत्यपुरोधसा।
नागोच्छ्वासप्रव्यथिता दैत्या: शुक्रेण सूचिता:॥
जग्मुस्ते पृष्ठतो लग्ना भीत: सोऽपि पलायित:।
दिशो दश दिवारात्रं द्वादशाहं प्रपीडित:॥
दैत्यैर्गृहीतस्तद्धस्तात्तेनापि पुनरेव स:।
अहं पिबेयं पूर्वन्तु न त्वञ्चेति विचुक्रुधु:॥
एवं विवदमानेषु काश्यपेषु सुधाग्रहे।
भगवान्मोहयित्वा तान्मोहिन्या व्यभजत्सुधाम्॥
विवादे काश्यपेयानां यत्र यत्रावनिस्थले।
कलशो न्यपतत्तत्र कुम्भपर्व तदोच्यते॥
गुर्विन्दर्कस्वपुत्रैश्च कुम्भोऽरक्षि निपातित:।
कलहाक्रान्तचेतोभिर्दैत्यै: शुक्रप्रचोदितै:॥

चन्द्रः प्रस्त्रवणाद्रक्षां सूर्यो विस्फोटनाद्धौ।
दैत्येभ्यश्च गुरू रक्षां शौरिर्देवेन्द्रजाद्भयात्॥
सूर्येन्दुगुरुसंयोगस्तद्राशौ यत्र वत्सरे।
सुधाकुम्भपूर्वे भूमौ कुम्भो भवति नान्यथा॥
देवानां द्वादशाहोभिमर्त्यैर्द्वादशवत्सरैः।
जायन्ते कुम्भपर्वाणि तथा द्वादश संख्यया॥
तत्राघनुत्तये नृणां चत्वारो भुवि भारते।
अष्टौ लोकान्तरे प्रोक्ता देवैर्गम्या न चेतरैः॥
तान्येति यः पुमान् योगे सोऽमृतत्वाय कल्पते।
देवा नमन्ति तत्रस्थान् यथा रङ्को धनाधिपान्॥
पृथिव्यां कुम्भयोगस्य चतुर्धा भेद उच्यते।
विष्णुद्वारे तीर्थराजेऽवन्त्यां गोदावरीतटे॥
सुधाविन्दुविनिक्षेपात्कुम्भपर्वेति विश्रुतम्॥

The verses for *kumbha yoga*

A translation of the following verses was presented in the second chapter.

Haridwar:

पद्मिनीनायके मेषे कुम्भराशिगते गुरौ।
गङ्गाद्वारे भवेद्योगः कुम्भनाम्ना तदोत्तमः॥

Prayaga:

मकरे च दिवानाथे वृषभे च बृहस्पतौ।
कुम्भयोगो भवेत्तत्र प्रयागे ह्यतिदुर्लभः॥

Ujjain:

मेषराशिं गते सूर्ये सिंहराशौ बृहस्पतौ।
उज्जयिन्यां भवेत्कुम्भः सदा मुक्तिप्रदायकः॥

Nashik-Tryambakeshwar:

सिंहराशिं गते सूर्ये सिंहराशौ बृहस्पतौ।
गोदावर्यां भवेत्कुम्भो भक्तिमुक्तिप्रदायकः॥

The verse for Ardha Kumbha

The following verse is cited by D. P. Dubey in *Kumbha Mela: Pilgrimage to the Greatest Cosmic Fair*. He heard it from Pt. Umarao Pandey who attributed it to the *Shakti-yamala Tantra*.

तदर्धे वर्षमाने तु कुम्भोर्ध्वं सार्धपञ्चकम् ।
अर्धकुम्भं विजानीयात्फलार्धं मोक्षदायकम् ॥

Verses from the *Ramacharitamanasa*

A translation of the below verses from the *Ramacharitamanasa* (2.105.3–8, 2.105) on King Prayaga was presented in the second chapter.

सचिव सत्य श्रद्धा प्रिय नारी । माधव सरिस मीत हितकारी ॥
चारि पदारथ भरा भँडारू । पुन्य प्रदेश देश अति चारू ॥
छेत्र अगम गढ़ गाढ़ सुहावा । सपनेहुँ नहिं प्रतिपच्छिन पावा ॥
सैन सकल तीरथ बर बीरा । कलुष अनीक दलन रनधीरा ॥
संगम सिंहासन सुठि सोहा । छत्र अछयबट मुनि मन मोहा ॥
चवँर जमुन अरु गंग तरंगा । देखि होहिं दुख दारिद भंगा ॥
सेवहिं सुकृती साधु शुचि पावहिं सब मनकाम ।
बंदी बेद पुरान गन कहहिं बिमल गुन ग्राम ॥

Verses from the *Mathamnaya Setu*

Descriptions of the *Dashanami* names as per the *Mathamnaya Setu* was given in the fourth chapter. The original verses from the work are as follows.

Tirtha and *Ashrama*:

त्रिवेणीसङ्गमे तीर्थे तत्त्वमस्यादिलक्षणे ।
स्नायात्तत्त्वार्थभावेन तीर्थनाम्ना स उच्यते ॥

आश्रमग्रहणे प्रौढ आशापाशविवर्जितः।
यातायातविनिर्मुक्त एतदाश्रमलक्षणम्॥

Vana and *Aranya*:

सुरम्ये निर्जने स्थाने वने वासं करोति यः।
आशाबन्धविनिर्मुक्तो वननामा स उच्यते॥
अरण्ये संस्थितो नित्यमानन्दे नन्दने वने।
त्यक्त्वा सर्वमिदं विश्वमारण्यं परिकीर्त्यते॥

Giri, *Parvata*, and *Sagara*:

वासो गिरिवने नित्यं गीताध्ययनतत्परः।
गम्भीराचलबुद्धिश्च गिरिनामा स उच्यते॥
वसन् पर्वतमूलेषु प्रौढं ज्ञानं बिभर्ति यः।
सारासारं विजानाति पर्वतः परिकीर्त्यते॥
तत्त्वसागरगम्भीरज्ञानरत्नपरिग्रहः।
मर्यादां वै न लङ्घेत सागरः परिकीर्त्यते॥

Sarasvati, *Bharati*, and *Puri*:

स्वरज्ञानरतो नित्यं स्वरवादी कवीश्वरः।
संसारसागरासारहन्तासौ हि सरस्वती॥
विद्याभरेण सम्पूर्णः सर्वभारं परित्यजन्।
दुःखभारं न जानाति भारती परिकीर्त्यते॥
ज्ञानतत्त्वेन सम्पूर्णः पूर्णतत्त्वपदे स्थितः।
परब्रह्मरतो नित्यं पुरीनामा स उच्यते॥

Magha-snana-vidhi in *Padma Purana*

A translation of the following verses from the *Padma Purana* (6.127.10–16, 44) was given in the fifth chapter. The verses are narrated by Dattatreya to Karttavirya (Sahasrarjuna).

अथातः संप्रवक्ष्यामि माघस्नानविधिं परम्॥
कर्त्तव्यो नियमः कश्चिद्व्रतरूपी नरोत्तमैः।
फलातिशयहेतोर्वै किंचिद्भोज्यं त्यजेद्बुधः॥
भूमौ शयीत होतव्यमाज्यं तिलविमिश्रितम्।
त्रिकालं चार्चयेद्विष्णुं वासुदेवं सनातनम्॥
दातव्यो दीपकोऽखण्डो देवमुद्दिश्य माधवम्।
इन्धनं कम्बलं वस्त्रमुपानत्कुङ्कुमं घृतम्॥
तैलं कार्पासकोष्ठं च तूलीं तूलवटीं पटीम्।
अन्नं चैव यथाशक्ति देयं माघे नराधिप॥
सुवर्णं रत्तिकामात्रं दद्याद्भेदविदे तथा।
तद्दानमक्षयं राजन् समुद्र इव सर्वदा॥
परस्याग्निं न सेवेत त्यजेच्चैव प्रतिग्रहम्।
माघान्ते भोजयेद्विप्रान्यथाशक्ति नराधिप॥

...

आकल्पसंचितं पापं जन्मभिर्यत्नरैर्नृप।
तद्ध्वेद्धस्मसान्माघे स्नातानां च सितासिते॥

Bibliography

The below list is not meant to be exhaustive and lists only the major sources I have used for research in this book. The numerous news sources that have been used are not listed.

Books

Dubey, D. P., ed. *Kumbha Mela: Pilgrimage to the Greatest Cosmic Fair*. Prayagraj: Society of Pilgrimage Studies, 2001.

Gautama, Siddhartha Shankara. सनातन संस्कृति का महापर्व: सिंहस्थ (in Hindi). Delhi: Prabhat Prakashan, 2016.

Gita Press (publisher). महाकुम्भ-पर्व (in Hindi). Gorakhpur: 2015.

Rai, Subas. *Kumbha Mela: History & Religion; Astronomy and Cosmobiology*. Varanasi: Ganga Kaveri Publishing House, 2001.

Tully, Mark. *The Kumbh Mela*. Varanasi: Indica Books, 2001.

Articles and reports

Baranwal, A., Anand, A., Singh, R., et al. "Managing the Earth's Biggest Mass Gathering Event and WASH Conditions: Maha Kumbh Mela (India)". *PLOS Currents Disasters*, 7. San Francisco, California: Public Library of Science, 2015.

Bihar State Disaster Management Authority (publisher). *Mass Gathering Event Management: A Case Study of MahaKumbh, 2013, Allahabad*. Patna: 2016.

Bryant, M. Darrol. "Dialogue at/with the Kumbha Mela".

Journal of Hindu-Christian Studies, 15 (9): 28–34. Notre Dame, Indiana: Society for Hindu-Christian Studies, 2002.

Dave, Shrirama. "साधुओं के अखाड़े: इतिहास और परम्पराएँ" (in Hindi). *Madhya Pradesh Sandesh*, Apr 2016: 118–127. Bhopal: Department Of Public Relations, Madhya Pradesh, 2016.

Information and Public Relations Department, Government of Uttar Pradesh (publisher). "प्रयागराज कुम्भ २०१९—कुम्भ मेला: एक परिचय". Lucknow: 2018.

Ministry of Health & Family Welfare, Government of India (publisher). *Setting-up of Mobile Telemedicine Unit in Kumbh Mela 2016 at Ujjain, Madhya Pradesh*. New Delhi: 2016.

Verma, A., Verma, M., Rahul, T. M., et al. "Acceptable trip distance for walking in mass religious gatherings: A case study of world's largest human gathering Kumbh Mela in Ujjain, India". *Sustainable Cities and Society*, 41: 505–512. Elsevier: 2018.

Verma, M., Verma, A., and Khurana, S. "Influence of Travel Motivation and Demographic Factors on Tourist Participation in World's Largest Mass Religious Gathering—The Kumbha Mela". *Prabandhan: Indian Journal of Management*, Aug 2018: 7–19. New Delhi: Associated Management Consultants Private Limited, 2018.

Documentaries

Buñuel, Diego (presenter). *Kumbh Mela—World's Biggest Festival*. Washington, D.C.: National Geographic, 2013.

Cohen, Ira (director). *Kings with Straw Mats*. 1986.

Disha TV (producer). *Discovery of Spiritual India: Kumbh,*

Digambar Akhara. New Delhi: 2016.

Feiler, Bruce (presenter). *Sacred Journeys With Bruce Feiler: Season 1, Episode 5 Kumbh Mela*. Arlington, Virginia: Public Broadcasting Service, 2014.

Jain, Harshit (director). *KUMBH-Eternal Journey of Indian Civilisation*. Indore: India Inspires, 2018.

Prabhatam Group (producer). *Know About Maha Nirvani Akhara, Know About Agni Akhara, Know About Atal Akhara, Know About Shri Panchayati Akhara Bada Udasin Nirwan*, and *Know About Shri Panchayati Udaseen Nirmal Akhara*. New Delhi: 2016.

Saregama Shakti (producer). *Mahakumbh Mela 2013: Moksha Ki Kamna*. Mumbai: 2013.

About the Author

Nityanand Misra, an IIM Bangalore graduate, is a finance professional working in the investment banking industry in Mumbai. At work, he specializes in quantitative finance, equity market microstructure, algorithmic trading, and execution consulting. Outside work, he is a multifaceted personality—a Sanskrit scholar, a polyglot, a grammarian, a littérateur, an instrumentalist, a musicologist, a researcher, an editor, an author, and a book designer. He is an alumnus of IIM Bangalore (2007) and a gold medalist from Gujarat University (2004).

Misra is passionate about Indic culture, especially classical and medieval literature, classical and folk music, and the traditional fine arts and performing arts. A disciple of Swami Ramabhadracharya, he is a scholar of Sanskrit and Hindi. He writes primarily on Hindu religion, scriptures (Vedas, *Purana*s, *Itihasa*s, etc.), philosophy, and culture.

Misra has authored thirteen books (including several bestsellers) and edited fifteen more in Sanskrit, Hindi, and English. His works have earned praise and from many dignitaries and scholars. He is also a professional onomasitician specializing in Sanskrit names.

Misra lives in Mumbai with his family.